FINITUDE, FEMINISM, AND FLOURISHING

Finitude, Feminism, and Flourishing

On Being Mortal, Like Everyone Else

Cristina L. H. Traina

2023 Madeleva Lecture in Spirituality

Paulist Press
New York / Mahwah, NJ

Book and cover design by Lynn Else

Library of Congress Control Number: 2023948871

ISBN 978-0-8091-5692-4 (paperback)
ISBN 978-0-8091-8856-7 (e-book)

Published by Paulist Press
997 Macarthur Boulevard
Mahwah, New Jersey 07430
www.paulistpress.com

Printed and bound in the
United States of America

CONTENTS

ACKNOWLEDGMENTS

All books are really the products of interdependent networks, and this one is no different. Profound thanks to the innumerable people who helped me to think about finitude for this project, among whom are Rachel Contos, Hille Haker, William Hutchison, Susan Ross, Kyle Stevenson, Anne Nicholson Weber, Thomas Weber, and Richard X III. The engaged, hospitable students, faculty, and faculty emeritae of St. Mary's College in Notre Dame have been on my mind as I have revised this argument; particular thanks are due to my wonderful colleagues Daniel Horan, OFM, and Julia Feder, who so generously organized the lecture on which this book is based. Donna Crilly of Paulist Press graciously extended deadlines when unanticipated events delayed completion. The Fordham College of Arts and Sciences and Department of Theology generously honored my finitude by sponsoring the leave that enabled me to think and write about it. For this particular project, my deepest thanks go to my foremothers in feminist theology as well as to the colleagues and students from whom I continue to learn it, only some of whom are mentioned in the footnotes.

I dedicate this book to the three people who have suffered most from my battles against finitude and who, despite that bad modeling, have become my guiding examples of flourishing within it: Catherine Hutchison, David Hutchison, and Margaret Hutchison Forrestall. The world will be a more just, less tragic place with you in it.

Luke Bretherton's *A Primer in Christian Ethics: Christ and the Struggle to Live Well* (New York: Cambridge University Press, 2023) appeared while this book was in press. It was impossible to engage it properly at that stage, but readers interested in finitude's implications for ethics are encouraged to consult it.

INTRODUCTION

Journalists who want to sum up contemporary women's lives succinctly choose photos: shots of middle-class women struggling to juggle children or elders or both with their household, work, and community responsibilities, and images of working-class women navigating all of that, plus public transportation and the bureaucratic puzzles they must solve in order to unlock affordable healthcare, housing, childcare, and other essentials. At all income levels they look tired, distracted, and stressed, with hair out of place and circles under their eyes. In other words, they are not flourishing.

Magazines and pop-up ads are also full of the solutions that our commercial culture suggests: planners to organize women's endless tasks, self-help books to help them prioritize and execute those tasks more efficiently, meditation and yoga classes, aromatherapy, proprietary exercise plans, house cleaning services, exercise, anxiety medication, nutrition supplements, massages, and spa days—all products that middle- and upper-class women can purchase as a means to feel better without taking anything off their to-do lists.[1] Working-class women are told that sacrifice, self-discipline, good humor, patience, and remembering that Jesus is with them at every step of the day will ease their paths at no charge.

It is hard to argue with these suggestions. Who would not feel calmer after a massage or a good laugh? Still, as solutions to overwork, they are problematic. First, because not everyone can afford the commercial ones, the richest women get the most relief. Second, both kinds of solutions imply that the problem lies with the woman, not the workload: if she were just more strategic, more patient, more energetic, calmer, and stronger, she would be able to handle it all with one hand tied behind her back. In other words, if she's not Superwoman already, she ought to step into the magic rays of a yellow sun and become her.

The many cohorts of U.S. Christian liberationist feminism—womanism, white liberal feminism, *mujerista* and Latina feminism, and queer feminism, just to name some—have agreed on this: women's problem is not that they refuse to access the superpowers that would help them manage their heavy loads effortlessly. Rather, strong, good, capable people who identify as women are victims of social injustice. It is not their fault that society demands a double shift—working for pay and caring for a household—or that they earn less than men for their paid work, cannot find affordable housing or reasonable childcare, are held to impossible standards of appearance, and endure sexual harassment.[2] Social, economic, and political structures are stacked against them. The solution is not spa days and planners. It's social change. If we can get rid of these systemic injustices, women will flourish. They will live healthy, balanced, happy, stress-free lives.

Accordingly, a largely white group of U.S. women theologians joined together in the 1960s, 1970s, and 1980s under the banner of feminism. They implied that if we could establish gender justice by demolishing patriarchy in society and the church, women's compressed and distressed spirits would expand to their full potential, channeling the divine and releasing untold creative power. Book titles and cover art celebrated the women's loving goddess energy, unleashed: for example, *Womanspirit Rising*, *Amazon Grace*, *Touching Our Strength: The Erotic as Power and the Love of God*, and *Journeys by Heart: A Christology of Erotic Power*.[3]

Many of these authors also believed that female oppression under patriarchy was the root oppression—the single thread that, if pulled, would bring all racism, ableism, and all other "-isms" and oppressive practices tumbling down. In contrast, woman-affirming theological movements that are alert to the ways in which sexism interacts with racism and other "-isms" disagree that sexism is the root of all gendered injustice. Instead, sexism and all other oppressions interact, placing women at intersections of injustices that interact in complex ways. For this reason, they have been hesitant to use the word *feminist*, at least without modification.[4] Still, they too have sought to undo injustice against women by expanding the dimensions of oppression that they work to correct.

Thus gender justice remains essential to every argument advocating women's flourishing, and for good reasons. It was—and is—high time that society and the church both nurtured and welcomed women's spiritualities, skills, and intellects. Definitely, women needed and still need to hear and repeat, "I am a child of God, filled with the power of the Spirit." Absolutely, women must believe in their full humanity, their abilities, their right to flourish. Without doubt, we must fight to erase gendered injustice. Increasingly, even white feminists have added that justice for women must be pursued intersectionally, by undoing not just structural sexism but also all the other interlocking "isms" that keep women down, including racism, ableism, and anti-immigrant policies and biases.

Yet across the spectrum feminist arguments for justice often overlook something: even if we could accomplish it, perfect social justice would not automatically create healthy, balanced, happy women—or men. We still would not be superheroes. We still would be finite. Although our spirits transcend time and space, we are, as the Book of Wisdom says, "mortal, like everyone else" (Wis 7:1). Even in a perfectly just world, we would undergo birth, childhood, aging, and death, not to mention physical and mental illness, disability, injury, and natural disasters. The paradox is that finitude—of which mortality is only a tiny sliver—is not a fault, not a shortcoming, not a failure of dedication and perseverance. As Elizabeth Johnson has argued, it is the divinely intended, good condition of our creatureliness.[5]

What do we do with the paradox that we are meant to flourish, but within divinely created boundaries of finitude that seem to make flourishing impossible? In a world that so obviously will be shot through with sin until the eschaton, musing about what finite human flourishing would look like in a sinless world seems to deflect energy from the urgent task of undoing sin's power to cause unjust suffering here and now. In addition, the various causes of suffering are almost impossible to unknit, in practice. Still, thinking within the limits of this finitude, guided by feminist methods, helps us to refine our vison of the just society we are pursuing. And while it does not solve the knotty moral problems of our day, it gives them a kind of nuance, texture, and specificity that can spark conversation across ideological divides.

The three chapters develop this argument in stages. Chapter 1 argues that even though most theologies that fall under the umbrella of feminism begin by assuming human finitude rather than addressing it explicitly, they contribute invaluable wisdom. Chapter 2 argues that beginning our theological anthropology with human finitude as a good, intended, created condition of our lives demands that we rethink what it means to flourish, even in a perfectly just culture. What is flourishing if not changeless perfection? What is autonomy if not complete independence? It ties these arguments to the doctrines of the incarnation and the Trinity, and it argues that the saints inspire us not because they are superheroes but because they are finite, fallible, and embedded in collaborative communities. Chapter 3 argues that centering flourishing-within-finitude in current, intractable moral debates over gender and pregnancy changes our framework for addressing them, moving promotion of interdependent community to the top of the ethical triage list. Along the way, I will argue that centering finitude strengthens rather than distracts us from feminist pursuit of justice in the world we have, a world that not only is finite but is beset by unjust oppression.

I

FEMINIST THEOLOGIES ON FINITUDE

Dependency and Limits

The feminist theologies referred to in the introduction embrace the liberationist belief that Christ's victory over sin promises more than salvation and future joy in heaven. In addition, this victory implies that when Christ returns, the power of sin in the world will finally be vanquished, and heaven will come to earth. In the meantime, the systemic forms that sin takes cause widespread suffering and injustice in all dimensions of life: interpersonal, but also political, psychological, economic, and cultural. Our job in the interim is to leverage the grace of the "already" of Christ's victory in the resurrection to uproot these sinful structures in preparation for the "not yet" of the second coming by advocating first for the welfare of the most oppressed.

Liberation theology holds that to do this we must first understand how these structures function; we need to get under the hood of the car, so to speak. Who better to do this than people who suffer most under injustice? They experience the workings of these powerful systems first-hand. According to liberationist feminism, women provide us with the first diagnosis of gendered oppression and thus the first clues to finitude. Feminist ethics of vulnerability, dependency, and limit round out the picture.

FINITUDE AT THE EDGES: U.S. FEMINIST THEOLOGIES OF LIBERATION

As Rosemary Radford Ruether said, "Feminism basically means the affirmation of the full humanity of women."[1] Christian feminist theologies are theologies that, at the very least, affirm women's full humanity alongside men's on the basis of women's and men's equal creation in the image of God: "God created humankind in his image, in the image of God he created them; male and female he created them" (Gen 1:26). Increasingly, they expand this claim to all genders' equal humanity and equal reflection of God's image.

White Feminist Liberation Theologies

U.S. white feminist theologians were the first to be admitted in significant numbers to the (until then) largely white male theological academy. In the 1970s and 1980s, U.S. white feminist theology drew on women's experience—primarily white women's experience—to describe oppressive patriarchal systems, to dislodge them, and to celebrate the power of the divine in women. The collections *Womanspirit Rising* and *Weaving the Visions* sifted Christianity, ancient myths, Native American practices, Judaism, Buddhism, Voudou, and other traditions for woman-empowering precedents.[2] For these authors, such precedents did not erase gender differences to create a single, generic way to be human. Instead, they celebrated what was divine and holy in women's embodied experience and mused that if women were created in the image of God, God must—in at least some respect—encompass the feminine as well as the masculine.[3] For instance, theologian Nelle Morton recounted how visualizing the Holy as Goddess transformed her struggles with a rare blood disease and particularly difficult menstruation from spiritual obstacles into spiritual pathways.[4]

Ruether is a classic example in the Roman Catholic tradition. Celebrating the sacred gift of the female body, reenvisioning God as Goddess or God/dess (as she wrote in *Sexism and God-Talk*), and reimagining spirituality, sacrament, and theology from women's perspective were central projects for her. Yet Ruether's aim was not to make women into men, but to free both from the sinful structures of patriarchy that bound men as well as women, even though they harmed women more. Ruether argued that stereotypically masculine qualities such as rationality, and purportedly feminine qualities such as emotional intelligence, were simply *human* qualities to which everyone should aspire.[5] With patriarchal limits removed, everyone could grow freely into balanced, fully realized human beings.

To be sure, not all of these authors embraced an androgynous ideal. For some, throwing off social patriarchy and ecclesiastical kyriarchy meant withdrawing from men and their practices and institutions to create entirely different societies focused on women's wisdom, gifts, and energies. For example, Mary Daly famously welcomed to her classes only people who both were born and identified as women, and lesbian philosopher Sarah Lucia Hoagland envisioned women-only communities that could experiment with nonhierarchical forms of feminist community away from the influence of oppressive patriarchalism.[6] For them, too, the point of seceding from male-dominated social structures was to develop women's nascent potential into fully realized personal creativity and power without reproducing oppression.

Still, these groundbreaking thinkers carried several liabilities. First, even when they also celebrated women's distinctive embodiment, these early white feminist theologians largely thought in gender binaries and, often treating (white) men's capacities and opportunities as the ideal, focused primarily on expanding women's capacities and opportunities to match them. Second, they tended to treat misogyny and structural sexism as root oppressions, marginalizing the experiences and arguments of feminists of color and oversimplifying their own analyses of injustice as a result. Finally, although Ruether and other white liberationist feminists did worry early on about *ecological* finitude and vulnerability, in their accounts *women's* potential—and therefore their capacity for orchestrating good outcomes when freed from patriarchal oppression—often seemed limitless.

Nevertheless, these thinkers took an essential step toward a theology of finitude by declaring that we are our bodies, and our bodies are ourselves; they are not merely containers for our infinite, untrammeled minds and spirits.[7] By largely embracing lesbianism, they also (perhaps inadvertently, in some cases) expanded our vision of gender and sexual identity beyond the binary precisely by tying it closely to our finite, personal experiences and embodied desires, warning us away from bodily gender determinism and toward greater attention to particularity.

Mujerista *and Latina Feminist Theologies*

Unlike early white feminist liberationists, *mujerista* and Latina feminist theologians have worked to establish justice at a multidimensional intersection of oppression.[8] For them, this intersection involves simultaneous subjugation along the axes of race, culture, gender, and often language and immigration status.[9] Ada María Isasi-Díaz tied the term *mujerista* to the argument that structures of oppression reveal themselves most clearly in the midst of Latina women's continuous struggle—*la lucha*—amid the challenges of the basic, embodied, everyday tasks—*lo cotidiano*—needed to keep themselves and their families going amid scarcity, unpredictability, and injustice.[10] Carmen Nanko-Fernández adds that "the daily encompasses the point of initial contact with the world as well as the milieu of ongoing engagement. It is configured by space, time, place, materiality, and proximity."[11] Life is the here-and-now of this day, this room, these particular people, and these concrete needs. Affirming the white feminist quip that the personal is the political, theorists of *lo cotidiano* point out that it is in shopping for dinner that one is confronted with the higher cost of food in an underserved neighborhood; it is in signing a lease that one comes face-to-face with the shortage of affordable housing; it is in leaving for work earlier and returning home later that one is faced with the unjust consequences of targeted cuts to public transit schedules.

Mujerista and Latina feminist theologians engage *lo cotidiano* as the first step in diagnosing and battling oppression; otherwise, as Nancy Pineda-Madrid says, what would be the point of their analysis?[12] Obstacles must be identified in order to be cleared, and modes of flourishing must be prioritized in order to be pursued. Still, the everyday needs of finite human beings most concern *mujerista* and Latina feminists not only because they are so all-absorbing and difficult to meet in an unjust world, but also because they would continue to be essential to human life even in a perfectly just world. In addition, they want to endorse the limited, concrete dailiness of each particular finite context as a site for theological reflection and source of theological vision. Finally, when we are not devoting all of our energy to sheer survival, pursuing our basic needs can be joyful as well as identity-preserving and community-building. For example, although we need to eat to survive, our means of doing that can also involve passing along positive inheritances: our families' longstanding foodways, and with them our happy memories of people, everyday comforts, and even religious traditions.

U.S. Womanist Theologies

Womanist theologians, too, work at the intersection of multiple historical oppressions, in their case racism and misogyny. Their focus, too, is liberation. And they, too, are concerned about concrete, daily survival. Yet, for two reasons they are more pessimistic, because more realistic, than twentieth-century white feminists and many Latina and *mujerista* feminists about the complexity and tenacity of oppression, and therefore they warn of the slow pace with which liberation is likely to occur. The first reason is their experience of enduring the especially violent structural evil of slavery and its aftermath as well as ongoing racism among supposedly liberationist white feminists and misogyny among self-described liberationist Black men. The second is their consequent insistence that, as activist and author Audre Lorde famously wrote, "The master's tools will never dismantle the master's house": critical methods that arise from racist, misogynist culture, including the historically white male discipline of Christian ethics, inevitably perpetuate racism and misogyny rather than undo them.[13] Womanist scholars insist that we must develop new critical tools for the long haul as well as new routes to flourishing.

Womanist scholars are especially helpful to conceptualizing both finitude and flourishing because of their attention to creative ways of thinking critically, flourishing robustly, and acting subversively amid the confines of ongoing, unjust oppression. Channeling anthropologist and author Zora Neale Hurston, Katie Geneva Cannon called this strategy "hitting a straight lick with a crooked stick." Methodologically, she noted, it required completely reconceiving Christian ethics through "the inclusion of Black women and the inclusion of Black women's moral reasoning"—which historically fell outside the formal discipline of Christian ethics—"within the structure of traditional ethics."[14] She accomplished this by drawing on Hurston—and others who fall outside Christian, white feminist, and Black male liberationist traditions—in search of virtues for surviving and resisting racist misogyny: invisible dignity, quiet grace, and unshouted courage.[15] These virtues are not repetitions of the virtues Christianity borrowed from Aristotelian philosophy but replacements for them that are to be exercised specifically in resistance to oppression. Thus, although Cannon used the language of inclusion, for her certifying womanist theology was not a matter of adding and stirring but of completely upending "traditional" Christian ethics by qualifying, recalibrating, or dethroning many of its claims and methods.

More recently, Emilie Townes has likewise neutralized racist and misogynist stereotypes of Black women by reappropriating these caricatures as critics who refuse the master's tools and as models of virtue under oppression. One example is the vocal, self-confident, truth-telling brashness of the stereotypical figure "Sapphire," "an image rooted in antifemale [and anti-Black] ideology and imagination." She is not only "loud-mouthed, strong-willed, sassy, and practical" but also "malicious, vicious, bitchy, loud, bawdy, domineering, and emasculating," intentionally unfeminine and nonmaternal. Although whites and Black men see the Sapphire character as dangerous because she is strong and independent as well as "not devoted to Whites" and unable to "be controlled by men," in Townes's womanist reading these are Sapphire's virtues. By turning the slur inside out and upside down, she creates a means of identifying and resisting misogyny and anti-Black racism and of flourishing as well as possible despite the unjust limits they artificially impose.[16]

Cannon and Townes are just two of the myriad womanist authors—like M. Shawn Copeland, Delores Williams, Diana Hayes, and Kelly Brown Douglas—who caution that dreaming an ethic of flourishing in finitude for an eschatological time to come is not our most pressing task. Even more urgently, we must pursue the two-pronged project of gradually dismantling injustice and imagining an ethic of resistance, creativity, and flourishing for the present and foreseeable earthly future, a future in which human injustice will continue to impose oppressive limits, particularly on people not gendered male and on people of color. This will require both abrasive, strong-willed brashness—to protest and destroy illegitimate, oppressive structures—and grace, dignity, and courage—to survive while they still exist.

Together, these liberationist feminists have something to teach us about finitude and flourishing in general, not just under oppression: we are embodied; our embodied selves have everyday needs, both individually and in community; and finding ways to flourish creatively within the constraints of our given needs can be an opportunity for ingenuity and joy in any case, and for imaginative subversion in unjust situations.[17] They also post enormous caution signs: unless we are vigilant, we will carry ingrained racism, misogyny, and other oppressive routines with us into our interpretation of these claims. Still, theologically, we can rest in the knowledge that this embodied finitude characterizes our good creation. This is the claim that underlies our moral obligation not just to meet others' needs but also to protest, resist, and unmake unjust systems that stand in the way of their flourishing—and our own.

DIVING DEEPER: VULNERABILITY, DEPENDENCY, AND LIMIT

These are the barest outlines of finitude. What does flourishing within them entail? Is it changeless perfection? Complete independence? Three nonliberationist strands of white Christian feminist ethics help us to round out an answer. We will focus on three representative authors: Hille Haker, Sandra Sullivan-Dunbar, and Deborah Creamer.

It is worth pausing for a moment to consider why U.S. feminist ethics of care and vulnerability seem to be primarily the province of white authors. In the late twentieth and early twenty-first centuries, white feminist ethicists have focused slightly more on the implications of social, political, and economic realities for justice in relations between individuals in their close relationships, and feminists of color more on the implications of these systemic realities for groups.[18] Another way to put it is that white feminist theologians and philosophers, who have not suffered under racism, have the "luxury" of meditating on the "essence" of care and care relationships in the abstract, then panning out to large-scale, gendered inequities in care and care work. For the liberal theologies and philosophies on which most white feminists of care depend lean toward individualism and toward isolating "care pairs" analytically from their larger systemic supports and oppressions. These theologies and philosophies also, not coincidentally, bear the taint of their colonial and racist origins. In contrast, feminists of color concentrate on the intersectional oppressions that make care virtually impossible to begin with.

It is true that defining "the person" in the abstract has typically been a colonial project intended specifically to bar some people from the category of "humanity." Likewise, defining "the relationship" in the abstract implies that social, political, and economic contexts are irrelevant to the ethics of intimate relationship, an error that John Paul II's theology of the body and its adherents also make.[19] We need to beware these invalidating mistakes. However, to the degree that the authors below struggle to define the human in order to expand rather than contract the category, and to account for rather than elide social pressures, they avoid these invalidating mistakes and can be useful to a constructive ethical project.

The Ethics of Vulnerability: Hille Haker

For Hille Haker, one of the most important consequences of finite embodiment is that we are vulnerable, "susceptible to be affected by incidents and/or conditions beyond [our] control" for better and for worse.[20] Whereas for feminist philosopher Judith Butler vulnerability is primarily precarity, for Haker vulnerability is part of our good, created, "basic openness to the world," the prerequisite for our coming into ourselves as human beings in relation with other beings and the world.[21] It comes in three varieties, all of which are connected to finitude.

First, as beings with limited powers and resources, we are ontologically vulnerable. Ontological vulnerability has to do with our organic dependence on the physical conditions of flourishing, which shape us, often permanently, through nurture, attack, or neglect. Second, as originally limited beings who need others' interaction and input to mature spiritually, intellectually, and emotionally, we are morally vulnerable. Moral vulnerability has to do with the risk our necessary, good openness and responsiveness to others entails for us as moral beings. We are susceptible to the respect, affirmation, and engagement that build our characters and also to the dismissal, domination, and misrecognition that warp them, often inexorably. Third, as beings who must live in interdependence with others both materially and socially, we are structurally vulnerable. Structural vulnerability is a product of our membership in complex social systems that position us at nexuses or intersections that either advantage us unfairly or unjustly jeopardize us both physically and existentially, not only depriving us of resources at critical points in our lives but also harming our agency and scope of action by diminishing our trust that society is a safe place for us to act.[22] As the poet Rita Dove says, one is "not born" wary but becomes so in response to "a torrent/of disregard."[23]

In addition to naming the vulnerabilities that arise from the finitude of this body, this community, and this society at this time in history, Haker's theory illuminates finite flourishing in two further ways. First, it rejects the individualism of some liberal political theory. We are social not as a second thought, like a contract we enter for convenience after having considered going it alone. We are social essentially: we can survive only amid relationships with other humans that nurture us or wound us, usually both. In addition, the combined distinctives of each person's life mirror their unique, particular creation: a person is inspirited and embodied in this physical setting, among these relationships, amid these structures.[24] Even though vulnerability is a human universal, in practice it is singular. To flourish is to live amid specific relations and structures that honor our physical and moral integrity and our agency, and through which we honor others' integrity and agency.

Care Ethics and Dependency: Sandra Sullivan-Dunbar

Liberationist feminism often points to caretaking as a time-consuming task that is invisible to economists but crucial to household economies and is usually performed by women, often by poor women of color, who are typically undercompensated or even uncompensated. For instance, a 2016 study found that across thirty-seven wealthy countries, women provided 75 percent of the childcare, and across most of the world, women took on the equivalent of ten extra weeks of unpaid care work annually.[25]

Liberationists would also see these phenomena as signs of structural injustice for women as well as for children; for example, the same study found that in "developing" countries, over 35 million children under five had no adult supervision for at least part of the week.[26] Philosophers and theologians of care point out that these injustices reveal basic qualities of our humanity. As feminist theologian Sandra Sullivan-Dunbar writes, care is a humanly indispensable, morally complex, deeply individualized practice necessary to thriving and even to survival for those receiving it. First, care involves a relationship between the carer and the cared-for that must respect the dignity of each, a dignity that cannot be rooted in rationality, agency, or any other non-universal human quality. Instead, it rests in our common, absolute, "primordial," creaturely dependence on God—which is to say, it rests in the fact that we would not exist at all without God's creation and God's continuous care and sustenance.[27] Second, as Haker also argues, human beings are not essentially self-sufficient and independent. Constitutionally, we are dependent not only on God but on one another. For much, most, and sometimes all of our lives, we need others' intensive, personalized care to thrive: in infancy, childhood, illness, injury, dementia, and decline, and even in everyday situations that are in some way beyond our ken but necessary to our welfare, from mentoring us in our work to teaching us the language of the country where we are living. Dependency is part of our created finitude, and care—from others practically and existentially and from God essentially—is indispensable to our flourishing.[28]

Disability Ethics, Limits, and Survivability: Deborah Creamer

So far, I have argued that our good creation entails our being essentially social, embodied, and in need of many things; existentially open and vulnerable; primordially and practically dependent; and ingeniously creative within these boundaries. These may not be earth-shattering observations. But feminist disability theologians take these claims to logical conclusions that may be less comfortable. They argue that liberationist and other strands of feminism are ableist when they imply that full liberation is not only freedom from interlocking structures of injustice and oppression, but also a return to a state of divinely intended natural beauty and mental, spiritual, and bodily perfection, including the erasure of all of one's disabilities, wounds, and illnesses—and maybe even pimples or wrinkles or muffin tops or gray hair.[29] What is more, they point out, salvation as liberation surely cannot demand the agency and capacity to participate in one's own liberatory process.[30] For instance, newborn children, many victims of severe strokes, and many people with profound intellectual disabilities cannot observe, analyze, and advocate for themselves. What are the alternatives?

First, much as Sullivan-Dunbar says of needing care, feminist disability theologians argue that we all spend much or most of our lives outside the range of "normal" abilities. As Jana Bennett writes, "we...have been lying to ourselves about having normal bodies (and minds)."[31] Even "nondisabled" bodies are neither ideal nor "normal": they leak, they hurt, they break down and have to go to physical therapy.[32] Complicating this observation even further is the fact that ability and disability are fundamentally queer categories, expanding and contracting according to whatever we currently happen to consider "normal" or "ideal." For example, whether attention deficit disorder is a disability or an alternative mode of productive functioning depends on the behavior and learning ideals that the dominant educational culture holds. Men have seen women's fertility as a disability, for decades opposing women's equal opportunity in hiring on the basis of their purported poor performance during menstruation and ignoring the creative boosts that come at other points in women's hormone cycles.[33] In addition, our embodied, inspirited selves defy the cultural ideals that produce standards of normality in the first place, revealing their contingency and fickleness. For example, consider how Western ideals of female beauty have changed and multiplied over time.

Deborah Creamer turns the tables, contributing significantly to our understanding of finite flourishing. She argues that if we abandon the impossible task of distinguishing disability from normality and stop defining disability as a deficit from normality, we can focus on what all human beings share: the unsurprising, universal experience of limits.[34] The social category of disability disappears, becoming simply "an intrinsic, unsurprising, and valuable element of human limitness."[35] This inversion of perspective, she says, calls "us to examine the values and choices involved in our attitudes toward limits."[36] That some of us have a limited ability to walk becomes less consequential if we realize that none of us can fly; that some of us are blind becomes less consequential if we realize that 75 percent of adults need some form of vision correction.[37] If we see these limits not as "signifying a lack or absence and emphasizing what cannot be done," not as "an array of unfortunate alternatives to omnipotence," but instead as "*good* or, at the very least, not evil" and "more positively [connoting] a quality of being,"[38] "we can then begin to move not only to a perspective where we embrace (value, accept, respect) the idea of having limits (as individuals and as communities)...but can also notice ways in which *these limits might embrace us*, acting to make and unmake issues of identity, relationality, space, and place."[39]

In this sense, she argues, limits "contribute to human identity, culture, and community."[40] To be sure, Creamer acknowledges that human limits that burden social participation still demand social and physical support, as a matter of justice.[41] She would not deny me my glasses, an IED victim a prosthetic leg, or a wheelchair user a curb cut. Her main point is theological: limits that are part of the embodied self "must be seen as integral elements of our understandings of self and other, as key characteristics for reflection in a theological anthropology," not as flaws to be eliminated.[42] If limits are integral to human being in general, our individual limits are integral to our individual beings. Womanists apply creativity and deadly serious whimsy within unjust, unchosen limits because their focus is liberation from oppression. But, as Creamer says, any unchosen limit is an invitation to creativity, to developing transcending practices of flourishing within its bounds. Sonnets or tweets (the old term for posts on the platform "X") are good analogies: tightly constrained containers that invite limitless ingenuity and even playfulness.

Embracing our limits does not imply that we can cease resisting unjust forces that create involuntary limits: industrial pollution that causes birth defects, wars and racist violence that result in disabling injuries, and many more that inextricably entangle injustice with the created finitude that it exploits, blurring the theoretical line between them. It also does not imply that we can wave the troublesome consequences of finitude away by, for example, simply removing disability from our cultural vocabulary and providing all the social supports needed to live well within the human limits that otherwise get in the way of flourishing. As disability theologian Nancy Eiesland wrote nearly three decades ago, we must live in the tension between bodily struggle and bodily affirmation:

> Embodiment is not a purely agreeable reality; it incorporates profound ambiguity—sometimes downright distress. There is simply no denying it. We concede the precarious position of living a difficult life and affirming our bodies as whole, good, and beautiful. In this incongruity, the revolutionary act of accepting our bodies as "survive-able," not deficient or deformed, is vital.... Instead of flagellating ourselves or aspiring to well-behaved "perfect" bodies, we savor the jumbled pleasure-pain that is our bodies. In a society where denial of our particular bodies and questing for a better body is "normal," respect for our own bodies is an act of resistance and liberation.[43]

As Mayra Rivera adds, the spirit and the flesh are intrinsically linked. The spirit of and in our finite flesh entails "the ambiguity of bodies that are ephemeral and tangible, fragmented and manifold, neither whole nor deficient," along with "pain, difficulty, and failure"[44]—which we can also "creatively transform."[45] Even in a sinless world, we would struggle with such inescapable finitude.

With this, Rivera has taken us back to the heart of our tradition, to the theology of the incarnation. But before we go there, a reprise: Our good, finite creation involves inspirited embodiment, with all its particularity and its limits—including mortality,[46] a limited supply of energy and waking hours, and the dailiness of ordinary needs. At every level from practical physicality through the emotional and intellectual to the spiritual, we are essentially vulnerable to others and dependent on them to keep us in being. Injustice preys on these qualities, but even in a perfectly just world, this finitude would be the basis of a survivable life—or, as Sullivan-Dunbar would say, a habitable life—filled with a complex joy and grief, hope and despair, physical pleasure and ease as well as physical pain and struggle that would bring with them possibilities for creativity, humor, and transcendence.[47] Flourishing is the interdependent life that we live within these limits by pressing against them on all sides, like climbers making our way up a crevasse, with a host of others whom we can count upon holding our safety lines.

Yet in a human, sinful world, systemic injustices impose formidable limits of another kind, limits that are all the more offensive for exploiting the very finitude and dependency that define our created humanity to begin with. For most people, finding their way to flourishing necessitates tricking, resisting, and undermining oppressive systems, strategies that pursue the two-pronged project of undoing injustice and thriving in the meantime. Affirming our good, created limits must support our obligation to use whatever power we have to identify and eradicate unjust ones.

II

INTERDEPENDENCE

Christology, Trinity, and Sainthood

In chapter 1, feminist critical reflection on embodied experience revalued finitude and limit as matters of our good creation. That anthropological insight becomes a lens through which we can reconsider central Christian doctrines: our belief in the *imago dei*, which says that all finite humans are created in God's image; the incarnation, which says that God became fully human in a particular person, Jesus Christ; the Trinity, which recognizes three persons in relation in one God; and the saints, who embody divine love in finite ways. All three land us back at the same classically feminist spot: flourishing as a matter of interdependent community.

THE *IMAGO DEI*

Christians believe that we are made in the image of God. We usually take this to mean that individual human beings each possess a single, God-given quality that imperfectly reflects something of God's essential nature. In recent centuries Roman Catholics have typically said that the *imago dei* resides in a person's reason, which is only partial now but will be complete, or perfect, when they individually know God face-to-face. This was a comfortable claim for twentieth-century neo-Thomist ethics because it dovetailed so nicely with the Enlightenment embrace of reason as the mark and measure of humanity.

The previous chapter challenges this idea in two ways. First, if all people lack reason for some of their lives, and some lack it for their entire lives, the *imago dei* must reside in some other quality.[1] It makes more sense to say that individuals participate intellectually in God's reason and wisdom to different degrees, but that God's essential nature is not, above and before all else, rational, and therefore neither is God's image in us. Second, it concluded that interdependence is the, or at least a, defining human quality. What happens to Christology, theology of Trinity, and our understanding of the saints if we begin with the idea that we image the infinite God not in our rationality but precisely in our finitude and interdependence?

CHRISTOLOGY

The paradoxical claim that finitude can mirror the infinite makes sense only because God lived among us as a finite (and thus finitely gendered) human being, Jesus Christ. The relationship between Christology, or what we believe about Jesus Christ (God as a top-to-toe human being), and theological anthropology (what we believe about humans in relationship with God) is dialectical: each affects the other. Who God is—self-revealed in a concrete, historical, embodied human being who was born, died, and was raised as we hope to be—says something about who we are—the sort of beings in whom God can be incarnated. Likewise, who we are, as persons, says something about how Christ can appear, and live, and die, and be reborn. But what shared human characteristic is most essential? There are many rich perspectives on this question. One comes from Daniel Horan: "loving the dust that we are."[2] Another is Susan Ross's description of us as the only beings we know who seek truth, goodness, and beauty.[3] Closer to the theme of this book is M. Shawn Copeland's description of the *imago dei* as our "capacity for communion with God," "a site of divine revelation," and a "basic human sacrament"—which we so often contradict and profane by abusing each other.[4] What light does finitude shed on this incarnational dialectic?

First, as theologians Hannah Bacon and Lisa Powell argue, "the flesh has always been part of the identity of

God" because "God's eternal being is always directed to incarnation": the infinite God determined God's own self to be essentially the-one-to-become-incarnate, to exist as a person in the finite human being, Jesus Christ, "eternally enfleshed, limited, and weak."[5] In addition to being born, eating, drinking, laughing, shouting, weeping, sleeping, and dying like any other finite person, as a human being Jesus Christ is finite—or as Sara Butler says, circumscribable—in particular ways.[6] He was said to be male, and not female or nonbinary or trans; his life covered a limited span; he was from Galilee, not Mongolia or North America or southern Africa; he spoke Aramaic; he was a person of color; he found crowds tiring; he lived under Roman oppression and died because of it; he faced his own death ambivalently.[7] And many details we cannot know: nearsightedness? Sexual orientation? Peanut allergy? Lisa Isherwood undoes our cultural "Jesus art" by musing that perhaps Jesus was fat.[8]

In addition, finitude and particularity dictate that God can be perfectly incarnate only in a specific, messy, breakable body. As Miguel Romero says, Thomas Aquinas thought that "the best and most fitting body for a human being" with respect to our end in God "is a body that is vulnerable to impairment, illness and injury." This vulnerability and the dependency that it generates are "essential creaturely goods" because a "perfect" or "invulnerable" body could not connect sensorially with the world, which is the pathway to learning and spiritual growth.[9] So for God truly to take up or receive universal humanity is paradoxically to embody the this-but-not-that particularities and the vulnerability to harm without which God would not be legible as a finite human.[10] In addition, a queer reading reminds us that some of those particularities belong to oppositions that are not given but culturally imposed, like race and gender, reinforcing the conclusion that Jesus Christ's maleness is an indicator of his human finitude rather than a reflection of God's infinite nature. Thus, the quality that matters to imaging God is that, like Jesus Christ, we are finite humans who lead our earthly lives in a relatively short span in particular, often distressing bodies, places, times, and cultural frameworks over which we have little control.[11] Full stop.

Second, Jesus Christ's divinity and humanity did not just coexist, like roommates, in the same body. Centuries of theological debate yielded the hypostatic union, the idea that divinity and humanity coexist in one person with one will. In other words, we can speak of two natures, but we cannot separate them; in Jesus they are not just compatible but inextricably entwined. As we saw in the first chapter, in recognition of "the incarnation's unfettered bond to our flesh" Mayra Rivera envisions spirit as intrinsic to flesh for ordinary humans as well, animating us across a distinction that is never a separation. As in Jesus, in whose image we are made, our spirit and our flesh are inextricably entwined. The fact that spirit-flesh is "the substance of our corporeality" implies that, just as for Jesus, our whole being is connected to, vulnerable to, limited by, and active in our physical and social worlds. And just as in Jesus, our whole being is also connected to the divine.[12]

If God opts out of fantastical, super-heroic existence in favor of finite life in the (wounded, limited, quirky) spirit-flesh, then spirit-flesh is also the mode of our *theosis*, or divinization—our opening ever wider to receiving and embodying divine love.[13] Orthodox Christians have especially nurtured the doctrine of *theosis*, and theologians across the Western theological spectrum have agreed that, particularly through the incarnation, Jesus Christ frees and enables "human beings to realize their original and highest vocation, which is to grow into the likeness of God and to participate in the fullness of life that God is, through the Holy Spirit" in a change that "will reach to the roots of our being."[14] If all of Jesus's finite, human particulars can embody the divine, ours can too, even if our particulars are different: like lighter or darker skin; the need for eight hours of sleep; residence in North America; subjection to systematic sexism and racism; menstruation, fibroids, fertility, or menopause. Because God became a finite human out of love and solidarity, each person in their particular finitude can grow in the Spirit and grace to channel God's love more fully.

Another implication of finitude is deadly risk. As Powell and Bacon point out, God's forever-orientation toward the finite and the fleshly is a perilous business. Perhaps no image expresses this risk more powerfully than iconographer Mark Doox's *Our Lady of Ferguson*, which chillingly transforms the *Platytera*—a classic icon of the infinite Christ in a finite human form within Mary's finite womb—into a foreshadowing of his violent and unjust death. Doox depicts Jesus as a target in silhouette, hands raised, in the crosshairs of a gun site, the site's target circle echoing his halo. In his finitude, Jesus is always already a potential victim of murder.[15] Indeed, there is no more convincing evidence of Jesus Christ's human susceptibility to human violence than the passion and the crucifixion. In the passion, God-in-flesh suffers human exhaustion; painful injuries from being beaten, whipped, and nailed to the cross; thirst while dying; the disappointment of betrayal in one sense by Judas, and in another by Peter; and desertion by many of his friends at his death.[16] A member of a network of Jewish communities that the Gospels describe as responding to Roman oppression in every possible way from resisting to collaborating, Jesus is portrayed as refusing to identify with any of them. Isolated by his unwillingness to seek shelter in a single political identity, he suffers the worst conceivable human violence.

And yet Jesus also rises bodily from the dead. As Nancy Eiesland points out, the second most remarkable thing about Jesus's resurrection—other than the fact that it occurred at all—is that he rises imperishable with his wounds, wounds that confirm his identity, wounds so large and gaping that Thomas can probe them with his fingers.[17] White feminist theology's early emphasis on restoration, health, wholeness, and beauty discouraged reckoning with these wounds. Yet if Jesus was incarnate in human flesh and rose to glory wounded, and we are created and rise in his image, then—as the author of the pseudepigraphical book 2 Baruch wrote—the restoration of the dead "shall make no change in their form," so that the living will recognize "those whom they now know."[18] Thus, as Powell and Copeland argue, even the perfection of our resurrected bodies will be marked by our quirks and the trials and violent injustices of our finite lives. Instead of ending our finitude and erasing our "marks" of particular, often unjust suffering, resurrection draws them into an eschatological reality in which they are no longer sources of pain but signs of "resistance and resilience" that we carry into community in Christ.[19]

One consequence of this theology of resurrection is the need to redefine earthly perfection to include every kind of finite, embodied self, not just physiques that fulfill cultural aesthetic ideals. Instead, our diverse and often troublesome bodies are the perfect vessels in which to grow close to God. And our scars—whether they are consequences of injustice or of luck—are integral to the only selves in which we can channel God's love.

Finally, perhaps even more to the point for ethics, we can say that precisely because God limitlessly embraced all of humanity by becoming a particular human, the incarnate Jesus Christ's scope of action was limited. In earthly life, Jesus Christ sometimes arrived too late, as for his friend Lazarus. He did not heal all the sick, preach to all the seeking, comfort all the grieving, or teach all the ignorant. Nor did his disciples. He advised them to shake the dust of unfriendly towns off their feet rather than to attempt to evangelize them. Likewise, he accomplished universal salvation, but not universal earthly freedom and flourishing. This produces a conundrum. To be part of the body of Christ is to be charged with realizing that daunting unfinished task, which seems to demand exactly the sort of superheroism from which Jesus, in his finitude, warns us away. To faithfully reflect the image of God revealed in Jesus is not to do everything ourselves, individually. We need to give ourselves a break.

But stopping there would leave us with therapeutic individualism. That true observation—we are finite, we cannot do it all—does not meet the needs of the people who will inevitably be left hurting if we do not at least try to do everything and help everyone. Jesus's practical finitude—his own inability to do it all—is not the end of the story: Jesus relied on his companions for evangelism, groceries, lodging, rides across lakes, relaying messages, donkey rental, Passover preparations, crowd control, and other tasks too numerous to mention. This leads us to the second mode in which we image God: Trinity.

THE TRINITY

The incarnation tells us how we reflect God as individuals: in the fleshly, temporal finitude that God takes on eternally in Jesus Christ. But as Suzanne Windley-Daoust argues, finitude is just the precondition for human relationship: without limits, without edges, there is no "where" from which to relate to a different other. She suggests that it is together, in dynamic relationships with one another, that we mirror God in the Trinity, the community of divine persons. Her examples, drawn from disability, emphasize dependence, mutual vulnerability, and mutual belonging—that is, interdependence.[20]

At one level, we can mirror the Trinity ethically by deploying interdependent relationships to supply solutions to the practical problems that arise from finitude: fixed resources, limited human capacities, our inability to do it all. Thus, following Paul, Deborah Creamer and Sarah Jean Barton argue that the body of Christ is composed of people with a vast variety of limits and abilities collaborating for the good of the whole.[21] For instance, Jeannine Hill Fletcher points to the "calculus of concern" through which those of us who care for others distribute "limited resources" under constraint and "at cost to [ourselves]"; like Jesus, we commit to relationships in finitude, vulnerability, and love, "willingly restraining" our vulnerable selves "in care for the vulnerable-other."[22] As Sandra Sullivan-Dunbar argued, the solution to the stress that this limitation creates lies beyond the individual: socially supported formal and informal networks of interdependence that supply all caretakers and those for whom they care.[23] Structures of justice resource and organize this support so that, like the mutually loving persons of the Trinity, we can promote each other's flourishing in face-to-face, interdependent networks of love. Conversely, when we close food pantries, or exclude some tornado victims from FEMA resources, or simply neglect to check on neighbors during a heat wave or a cold snap, we sever the networks of interdependence that make possible both care and our reflection of the Trinity.

As these examples hint, however, our theology of Trinity makes all the difference to our understanding of the *imago dei* we corporately embody in this ethical interdependence. Feminist theologians such as Sarah Coakley and Susan Abraham warn us away from swirly pastel images of the Trinity as Divine Persons in eternally balanced relationships of egalitarian mutuality. Rather, they invite us back to hierarchies, understood as "dynamic systems that organize themselves around individual gifts of complex selves" in which one, then another, exerts power and agency.[24] If Trinity is an ever-shifting, dynamic hierarchy among Creator, Christ, and Spirit, so will our imperfect reflection of it be.

Almost all relationships of care exhibit this uneven, dynamic quality. Care for children is the usual example, but Mary Jo Iozzio reflects on how, when her father developed dementia, he shifted from vibrantly collaborating in her family's interdependent welfare to almost exclusively receiving care from them. Iozzio writes that the interdependent "model of the Trinity presents a paradigm of the interdependent nature of human existence."[25] Patterns of relationship changed in Iozzio's family as her mother activated her own network of interdependent connections, such as "visits with her sisters, and communion visits to parishioners unable to attend weekly services"[26] as well as new relationships with adult daycare providers, "home health aides from hospice, the Veterans' Administration, the County Office on Aging, and a private duty contract" nurse. Iozzio also muses that her father needed others' patience, fidelity, humor, and stories just to preserve his identity and his freedom.[27] As Richard Holton says, quite literally, "Keeping a personality going in dementia, demanding as that is, is a job for us all."[28] Like the members of the Trinity, interdependent humans are rarely functioning at equal strength at any given instant. Activity and reception occur in changing configurations. Imaging God as Trinity means continually engaging wider, dynamic relationships of interdependence, both informal and institutional, to ensure flourishing.

The example of keeping another person's personality alive in dementia suggests that we image the Trinity not just ethically, through dynamic networks of justice and love, but also existentially. Trinitarian doctrine often feels mathematical: three persons in one God—Creator, Christ, Holy Spirit—none of whom can exist without the other.[29] Yet they are not only interdependent among themselves, internally and, with the world, externally—one creating, one redeeming, and one sanctifying—but they are also perichoretic—

mutually participatory. Within each, the others also dwell. Scratch the surface of one, and you will find the other two. We image the Trinity in this sense as well; scratch our surface, and you will find all the people who dwell in us. For Haker, as we saw, because we are intrinsically social and open to others—the word *person* includes the individual with their social relations—our vulnerability means that we are partly the products of our relationships, for better or worse, physically, emotionally, and politically. Likewise, for Mayra Rivera, "the multiplicity of relationships that constitute" us mark us indelibly in the spirit-flesh, "incorporating the familiar *and* the unknown, the visible *and* the invisible, the nurturing *and* the oppressive."[30] Others reside at the core of our existence, and we reside at theirs.[31]

In the sense that imaging the Trinity means dwelling in one another in love, imaging the Trinity means flourishing in one another. Likewise, an attack on someone to whom we are closely related does not merely reverberate through the network of practical interdependence but is also an existential attack on all. We are literally part of one another, and others are part of us; as St. Paul says, we are "members of one another" in the Body of Christ (Rom 12:5). We owe it to one another to keep one another's identities, stories, and personalities going. We owe it to one another to honor not just the vulnerable selves that we are individually but also the networks that create and support us. Cutting us off from our network—leaving us housebound or in prison, arbitrarily removing us from our parents, or forcing us to migrate to stay alive—harms us not just by disrespecting our individual origin and end in God, which is bad enough, but also by slicing away the others whom we need to flourish in our ordinary, good, created finitude, the others who are literally *part of us*—not to mention harming them by removing us from the networks on which they rely. To respect finitude is precisely to respect connection and interdependence as essential to our being, materially, emotionally, and spiritually, and to respect the connections themselves.

Finally, the Trinity has eschatological significance. If, as Powell and Copeland insist, the marks of our earthly life follow us into the reign of God, this means that our resurrected life does not bestow physical wholeness or independence or self-sufficiency or infinitude. We can flourish—our wounds and ills can cease troubling us—only if we continue to minister to one another. Thus, as Powell suggests, perhaps this "foundational, original" "dependency and vulnerable need...is...perfected in the reign of God as absolute interdependency."[32] Rather than being a place of rest, the future reign is a dynamic condition of universal flourishing, with loving generosity flowing eternally in endless anticipatory response to one another's needs.[33] We grow more completely into the image of God as we corporately, eternally perfect our interdependence—an interdependence in which our diverse needs and strengths remain rather than being washed away.

This is why Jeannine Hill Fletcher can say, "our lives are not altogether our own"—others are caught up in ours, and we in theirs.[34] And this perhaps is why Nancy Eiesland could say that "our bodies participate in the imago Dei, not in spite of our impairments and contingencies, but through them."[35] Resurrected life mirrors trinitarian mutuality not in establishing homogeneity among us but in making difference and even unjust injury the path to individual and communal, perichoretic flourishing. Imaging the Trinity is a group activity, by definition.

RECONSIDERING THE SAINTS

Christology and theology of the Trinity lay the theological foundations for interdependent, perichoretic relationship in the spirit-flesh. A slight detour may help to connect this abstract theological speculation with the concrete moral reflection of the next chapter. It is a counterintuitive side trip for a feminist brought up in the 1960s and 1970s: the saints. Raised by a Presbyterian convert mother and an intellectual father who saw his Sicilian grandmother's devotions to the saints as superstitious, I grew up with a social justice version of Vatican II Catholicism not just bereft of statues and rosaries but downright suspicious of them. I think what bothered my father most about my great-grandmother's devotions was the tinge of magical superheroism he thought she attached to them: at her bidding, she believed, they performed small but still superhuman miracles such as finding lost objects or bringing good weather. I was well into my twenties before I encountered Orthodox Christian devotion to the saints through icons and began to realize that in her friendship with her patron saints my *bisnonna* had been onto something important: throughout Christian history we have not only recognized people who have palpably embodied limit-transcending divine love within the finite boundaries of their lifetimes, eras, capacities, places, vocations, and genders, but we have been inspired by them and felt connected with them, too.[36] They remind us not only that holiness is possible in the flesh, but that it is impossible anywhere else.

One aid to friendship and inspiration has been icons, devotional portrayals of Christ and the saints. Since Christianity's early days, icons have been both inspirations to holiness and signs of the Divine incarnate in the concrete, imperfect particularity of finite, historical, material people. As Greek Orthodox scholar Spyridoula Athanasopoulou-Kypriou writes, icons inspire through their "inclusivity and their emphasis on the historical reality, on the uniqueness of all beings, male and female and on the exceptional story of each person/saint."[37] Athanasopoulou-Kypriou is interested in the implication that women saints embody the holy not in spite of their gender but precisely as women.[38] By the same logic, this is true of all elements of saints' finite humanity. Thus, iconographers typically ground saints in their times and biographies, including props that remind viewers of their stories: for example, the scholar and spiritual writer St. Teresa of Ávila is usually pictured with a pen or a scroll.

In addition to depicting the saints in all their particularity and finitude, iconographers facilitate connection by making them truly contemporaneous to the viewer. Although Orthodox iconographers generally place saints in abstractly sketched settings suggesting the saints' periods, the strong, detailed focus on the foregrounded figures emphasizes their eternal, universal significance. For similar reasons, Western iconographers have often transported historical saints to their present day. Robert Lenz, OFM, paints Byzantine-style icons of contemporary religious figures and of established saints reimagined in all races and cultural settings. Painter Gracie Morbitzer depicts "the saints with character, correct age, and ethnicity and modern style to show how amazing, human, and just like us they were. In turn, they show us we can be just like them."[39] Her often shockingly young subjects (why do we often think of saints as old and wizened?) look as if they could pass us on the street, incognito—which is her point. St. Anne sports a striped t-shirt; St. Augustine rocks an Afro; a foppish, polo-clad St. Ignatius of Loyola contemplates a book, pen in hand.[40] Even the now laughably anachronistic dress of some medieval and Renaissance Western depictions of saints once reminded their contemporary viewers that they too could open themselves to the Spirit within the limits of their finitude in their own place and time.

Icons also point toward two particularly Christian forms of interdependent flourishing: the communion *of* saints and communion *with* saints. The communion *of* saints that Christians affirm in the Nicene Creed is the belief that the community of the faithful extends backward in time, including all who have gone before and now reside with God. Theologian Elizabeth Johnson writes of the communion of "all living persons of truth and love" with each other and the saints of the past. This transcendent communion among finite persons of past and present dissolves the imagined physical boundary dividing heaven from earth and accordions the temporal distance between us.[41] Orthodox Christians reinforce the union of heaven and earth in one interdependent community of saints in the Divine Liturgy by filling their churches with sometimes dizzying numbers of icons, who manifest this communion palpably.

Like my Sicilian great-grandmother, we can also commune *with* saints. As Orthodox theologian Andrew Louth says, icons of the saints with symbols of their charisms "mediate to us the presence of those to whom we pray," bringing us into intimate connection with these other finite persons who nevertheless symbolize and channel the transcendent.[42] Once again, the holy is manifest in the concrete, and once again, flourishing is a matter of interdependent relationship—not just in time but also across it.

Contemplating the saints also brings us into the presence of their communities of interdependence. Like the Jesus of the Gospels, the saints do not act alone. They have retinues. For instance, St. Teresa of Ávila not only wrote spiritual works that have inspired generations of Christians but also founded seventeen monasteries and helped her friend and sidekick, St. John of the Cross, reform the Carmelite men's order.[43] Alongside her worked not only St. John but at least seventeen abbesses and, surely, countless nuns who cared for her in her constant ill health. Dorothy Day relied on visionary friend Peter Maurin, the good graces (and at times mere tolerance) of the New York Catholic archdiocese, and thousands of funders and volunteers who to this day have kept her vision of hospitality alive.[44] Paradoxically even the hermit saints ended up with collaborators, often creating communities in spite of themselves by either mentoring and guiding contemporaries or inspiring later generations.

Reading this interdependence from the other side suggests that saints' sanctity is in large part their ability to inspire their collaborators to embody the love of God, their ability to call others to holiness-in-finitude. Thus, Peter Mena argues that when we read hagiographies—pious biographies—of saints, we should turn the camera from the saints they exalt to the communities that surround them. For example, reading the life of St. Syncletica through the lenses of Gloria Anzaldúa and Cherríe Moraga, he suggests that interpreting the suffering saint's holiness as a matter of her individual heroism in a struggle with illness misses much of the point. Rather, "Syncletica's body becomes the catalyst for constructing a communal sense of identity in which all those who care for her participate in the production of such holiness."[45] From this perspective, a person's saintliness—connected to their *theosis*, or divinization—emerges in interdependence with a concrete community that in turn grows in God's love through its specific response to the saint and thus, reciprocally, determines the saint's identity for eternity. As iconographer Fr. Stamatis Skliris has written,

> In [their] eschatological form, every person will possess those characteristics that constitute the identity bestowed on [them] by the community within which [they] developed the temporal relationships (of love, unit, sacrifice for others and so on) which are necessary in order to attain to the eschatological mode of existence.[46]

Saints, in other words, are less superheroes than close-at-hand models of interdependent, communal flourishing on both the spiritual and practical planes. We cannot conceive of their saintliness—their opening to the divine—without the communities of people in whom they dwell, and who dwell in them.

In a final encouragement to ordinary humans, they, too, are ordinary. They have personality faults, as we do. The Acts of the Apostles and even his own letters depict St. Paul as stubborn, argumentative, judgmental, and presumptuous—and that's before we consider his initial zealous persecution of Christ's followers. Their failures to transcend the worldviews of their own times have led them to harm others brutally, just as posterity will say of us: witness St. Junipero Serra's de facto enslavement of native people or champion of native rights St. Bartolomé de las Casas's suggestion that colonizers should free unjustly indentured Latin American and Caribbean native people and enslave Africans instead. Both Mother Teresa of Calcutta and Dorothy Day were accused of failing to provide adequate care to the unhoused people they served.

Day and Mother Teresa are also reminders that, like everyone else, saints constantly make difficult calls in tough circumstances with limited resources in an unquestioning attempt to lessen the unpostponable need of people standing before them. This is another lesson for ethics: our need, finitude, and mortality mean that immediate necessity cannot always wait for a study to assess causes, a grant application, a new program, and a new staff. It also cannot wait for wars to cease, the climate to improve, racism and classism and depressions to end—in short, for the ideal world to appear. Saints like Day and Mother Teresa gather collaborators to lovingly if imperfectly extend the net of interdependence over people whom we have unjustly severed from it, restoring their dignity and inching them closer to true flourishing. This alone is enough for us to see the Spirit working in them and believe that it can work in us, without suspending the critique that pushes us to embody justice and compassion ever more perfectly.

The saints remind us concretely that we image the divine individually in our particular, wounded, vulnerable finitude; we image it corporately in flourishing, interdependent, dynamic, perichoretic interdependence across space and time; and we do both imperfectly in an imperfect world, inspired by the friendship and example of fellow travelers across time. What does this mean for ethics, for the call to flourish together in finitude amid injustice and destruction?

III

FINITUDE, GENDER, AND PREGNANCY

The previous two chapters have argued that even if we could end oppression and injustice—even if we could, as M. Shawn Copeland says, remove evil "physical, mental, emotional, and spiritual forces" that we apprehend "as jeopardizing [our] very existence"—flourishing within the limits of our created finitude would be too messy for TikTok and Instagram.[1] Certainly, we would have the resources and relationships adequate to collaboratively transform our own and others' limits from barriers to platforms for creativity and connection. Still, rather than a series of air-brushed poses, a just, finite life would be a dynamic, nonperfectionistic movement of our spirit-flesh amid Rivera's "ambiguities of bodies that are ephemeral and tangible, fragmented and manifold, neither whole nor deficient."[2] Neither would flourishing be a matter of unconstrained freedom or arbitrarily chosen identity, for it would still entail operating within the constraints of birth, responsibility for others' care, pain, grief, mental and bodily illness, disability, death, others' ongoing formation of us, and our ongoing formation of them. Neither would it imply independence. There would be no icons of purportedly self-sufficient saints. Rather, like the Orthodox icon of Mary and Elizabeth joyfully supporting each other in their miraculous yet daunting pregnancies, picture frames would be crowded with evidence of our interdependence and mutual indwelling.[3] For, as Rivera argues, it is exactly in our ordinary dailiness, "in the transient events of finite, vulnerable existence [that] the spirit-flesh makes possible the transfiguration of our wounds and the incarnation of improbable hopes."[4]

Although perfect justice is a matter of eschatological grace, reflecting on the shape finite flourishing would take in such a world is not a pointless exercise. Rather, beginning with good, created, interdependent finitude calibrates our moral approach to life in this still sinful world. It reminds us to aim for interdependence rather than Instagram, and for compassion rather than compliance.

Four points seem especially important. First, we are finite in time; we are "mortal, like everyone else" (Wis 7:1). In the United States, our lifespan averages 79.1 years for women—less than that for white, Black, and Native American women—and 73.2 years for men.[5] We care for ourselves and each other within this frustratingly short horizon. Womanist and Latina feminist scholars are correct: The long and necessary project of chipping away at structural evil cannot eclipse the immediate needs of finite people who are suffering under injustice now, and who have no time to waste. We must urgently seek and promote flourishing within this short span and its tangle of created, cultural, and unjust limits even as we simultaneously work to identify and dismantle the unjust ones. In addition, our finitude installs us in specific times, places, and cultures that fill us with assumptions and present us with finite scopes of action. We may transcend our place and time in some ways, but we will never escape it for a generic, ideal world. We must live our lives in this one.

Second, our mortality is not just a matter of a finite span of years; we are also finite in our spirit-flesh, which entails needs that must be met within almost infinitesimal spans of time and which offers no "rewind" button that allows us to go back and make up for a past harm or a lack. As infants and young children, we undergo delicate neural development that lays the foundation for our physical, intellectual, and emotional welfare and cannot be compensated if it is interrupted by malnutrition, neglect, or abuse. As pregnant or laboring or miscarrying or postpartum women, we may die if we do not receive the medical care that we need, right now, today. We are vulnerable to psychological and spiritual traumas that we cannot uproot from our spirit-flesh. In prison, we may die when staff withhold basic medical care and medications. We are also susceptible to physical injuries and illnesses that can harm us permanently. This dimension of our finitude intensifies our immediate claims on one another, shifting our emphasis in ethics from evaluating an individual actor's success or failure at generically "doing enough" for others over the course of their lives to honoring the urgency of our unending ontological interdependence.

Third, as Margaret Farley argues, mortality and finitude entail epistemic humility.[6] Because we are finite, we cannot know everything. And yet, we must seek holistic flourishing. This leads to a paradox. On one hand, our knowledge is always provisional; we must approach every new situation with genuine curiosity; and even when the path seems well established, we must not just hold a space for new information but actively seek it, entertaining unexpected ideas. This includes being open to practices we would not have to consider employing in a perfect universe: undermining, resisting, or ignoring unjust institutions, for example, or responding violently to violence.[7] On the other hand, incomplete knowledge does not excuse inaction. We must do the best we can with the knowledge we can reasonably acquire. The urgency born of our own and others' finitude demands that we act with decently informed boldness rather than a paralyzing degree of caution. Because we cannot wait to act until we know everything, our attempts will yield imperfect results, our provisional strategies will change in response to new information, and flourishing will be a moving target. Just as temporal finitude shifts the evaluative focus from individual actors' won-loss records to the needs that must be met, epistemic finitude shifts the focus of ethics from identifying the correct norm to ensuring an open-ended process of discernment.

Amid this reflection, upholding individual civil rights and individual welfare is imperative, for naming rights is a prerequisite for making strong justice claims in a fundamentally unjust democratic society. Still—and this is the fourth point—the best guarantee of these rights is something far more basic: just, dynamic networks of interdependence at every level from the interpersonal to the global. Flourishing in finitude is not solely about individuals' welfare, measured by discrete benchmarks; it arises from interdependent community, which deserves promotion and protection in itself. If we are nurturing such networks, we are honoring created finitude. This also means that the mode of our interdependence is as essential as its shape. If we are in a position to shape a community, the "how" of compassion and epistemic humility must determine the "what" of the structure or policy that emerges—even if, as we will see, compassion sometimes entails resistance or even violence of a kind.

In essence, putting finitude—our mortality, daily necessities, location in time and space, critically timed requirements, epistemic humility, and compassionate, just, dynamic interdependence—first forces us to pan out from current ethical squabbles and reconsider the priorities that drive moral reflection. A reader who picks this book up in the future will have other moral impasses in mind, but at the time of this writing conflicts around gender and pregnancy are among the most urgent.

GENDER

Taking finitude seriously affects our aims in moral reflection, which in turn affect our methods of discernment. For instance, in recent decades official organs of the Roman Catholic Church at all levels from parish to the Vatican have treated ethics as the discernment of norms or rules that define the boundary between definitely sinful and potentially virtuous behavior. It is true that Vatican consistories, the United States Council of Catholic Bishops (USCCB), and even some diocesan documents addressing sex and gender have echoed feminist theology in embracing an integral, social, nondualistic image of created finitude. Yet they have done so in a particular key, elevating a single element of our finitude above all others in an effort to create a universal behavioral norm. They argue that God clearly revealed our given sex organs as physical signs of two essentially different bodily, mental, social, and spiritual ways of being in the world. Consequently, they say, we must honor the limits that these good, divinely created realities of sex and gender impose on social and medical innovation. In short, according to this argument, a person's mental and spiritual gender is firmly yoked to the sex organs with which they were born and constitutes a limit that must never be denied or crossed. What is more, transgressing this norm harms church and society by upending the sacramental and family structures at their respective cores. Thus, from this point of view claiming a trans* or nonbinary identity can be only a sinful or, at best, mistaken rejection of this finite, good, divinely created, integral, gendered nature.[8]

According to the feminist theological anthropology developed here, our sex organs are not the most basic sign of our created finitude, nor do they define two separate varieties of human nature. If these claims were true, it would be impossible for the *imago dei* to reside both fully and equally in people of both genders. These claims also contravene the evidence: people's anatomy does not always match even their genetic sexual profile, let alone their self-understandings. In addition, gendered norms of behavior vary among and within cultures, belying the idea that there are essential, universal feminine and masculine ways of thinking, feeling, and acting.[9] Opting instead for the vision of the *imago dei* developed here implies, first of all, that our finitude, interdependence, mutual indwelling, and communion across time and space are far more basic to our embodied reflection of God's image than our apparent physical gender. For this reason, Elizabeth Johnson argued decades ago, Christian feminist theology has embraced "one human nature celebrated in an interdependence of multiple differences."[10] Opting for finitude has even more thoroughgoing methodological implications, however. If our knowledge is finite and constrained by our experience and standpoint, our first tasks in ethics are not the determination of gendered norms but the perfection of virtues: epistemic humility, active curiosity, and promotion of interdependent community.

Epistemic humility is an indispensable virtue for addressing contested questions that bear directly on finite flourishing. As feminist theologians of all stripes have said for decades, people who suffer from any sort of oppression or marginalization are experts on their own lives and the forces that bear down on them. In general, as anyone comes to know her own particulars in community and over time, she learns what she needs to flourish within these boundaries. But we tend to have parallax when it comes to others' lives, especially if we do not share their particularities and limits. If we want to know what another person's finite, interdependent flourishing requires—in *this* world at *this* time—we should ask. We would not think of refusing, much less disbelieving, someone who replied, "Stand by my good ear," or "Print my exam in 16-point font," or "Sit down to speak with me when I'm in my wheelchair," or "No gluten, I have celiac disease," or "Watching footage of police brutality gives me nightmares," or—like Jesus on the cross, "I thirst." Questions of gender identity are no different.

Epistemic humility also reminds us that, as finite beings located in particular times and spaces, we do not and never will inhabit a pure or generic social or religious universe. Our contexts strongly flavor our assumptions, our methods of reasoning, and the dynamics of our interdependent relationships. With respect to gender and sexuality, our cultural practices are distinctive, often rigid, and in many ways arbitrary. In the United States of the 2020s, a suit with pants is "professional" wear for a woman, but a man who wears a dress is "in drag," taken seriously only in the context of artistic or political performance. These inflexible but arbitrary standards—for instance, this author's school forbade her to wear the now-almost-required pants until she was in the fifth grade—literally sideline people who do not feel at home in them. For their sake, and as a matter of the epistemic humility our created finitude demands, we must always be ready to reconsider our understandings of gender and the social practices that we take as routine, even when those practices and understandings are expressed theologically. Absent any strong contradictory indications, we should ask with genuine curiosity, believe the answers, and respond as well as we can.[11]

Reflecting on created finitude also encourages us to make dynamic interdependence, which minimizes the costs of our finitude and maximizes the likeness of the Trinity among us, a test of our moral reasoning. Here, the current official Catholic approach to gender falls short. For someone who hungers for the integral social, physical, spiritual, intellectual gender coherence that Roman Catholic teaching promotes but finds their finite body and social identity at odds with their given mind and spirit, existing gendered social networks of interdependence are more wounding than sustaining. The logical but tragic response for such a person is to break from them, seceding from community or, in the worst case, from life itself.

For those who survive it, secession not only removes them from their networks of support but also deprives the community of their contributions, weakening both the common network of practical interdependence and their relationships of mutual indwelling. The solution that the Vatican and U.S. bishops propose is conversion to the social and ecclesial roles that currently come with their given sex, as a condition of full reincorporation into the community. Even Pope Francis's recent insistence that a trans* person can serve as a godparent and his overtures to trans* women simply imply that trans* persons' refusal of their created, physical nature is a sin no worse than greed, pride, or any number of others that dog any serious Christian on their journey toward greater holiness.[12] Yet this approach transgresses epistemic humility, disrespects the person by dismissing their account of their own experience, and puts the onus of connection on the one who is already suffering in isolation and perhaps under persecution, not to mention continuing to iconize culturally specific ideas of gender.

Prioritizing common, finite interdependence requires activating the alternative: expanding and transforming the network of interdependence on conditions that trans* and nonbinary people set. We do this already when we add reparations—which return wealth and power to those from whom it was unjustly taken, for use on their terms—to affirmative action—which issues invitations to individual underrepresented persons from powerful institutions, on the institutions' terms. We do this already when we design buildings that are universally accessible rather than creating separate pathways for people with physical disabilities. As Sullivan-Dunbar argues, we could do this if we asked care providers what support they needed rather than presuming—or even more radically, if we asked those for whom they care.[13]

In a similar transformative shift of perspective, we can loosen both our strongly binary vision of gender and the prescriptive connection between the physical body in which a person is born and their gender identity.[14] Although gatekeepers may be unsettled by the unfamiliar practice of revising the conditions of interdependency on terms set by the very people whom they themselves had previously excluded, the gatekeepers' discomfort hardly registers on a scale calibrated by others' right to flourish at all. Just as importantly, as with reparations and universal design, holding apparent bodily gender loosely ensures that everyone participates robustly in the network of interdependence on which we all depend and that is weakened by anyone's absence. People who are white, or able-bodied, or cisgendered should embrace all these shifts of power and perspective out of self-interest, if for no other reason. It is an argument from the common good, beginning with finitude rather than with gendered social organization.

Finitude also tunes our responses by reminding us of the urgency of mortality. If we want to honor our current siblings' finitude, we do not have the luxury of waiting several generations to discern how to promote individual, gendered flourishing amid robust, concrete interdependence. A mortal person who wants to transcend gender stereotypes by developing the full spectrum of supposedly gendered capacities and virtues cannot delay for a couple of centuries in the hope that society will eventually adopt Rosemary Radford Ruether's androgynous gender ideals.[15] They need to flourish and to contribute within their lifetime, perhaps in the formal social space that a nonbinary identity provides. Likewise, for a person with sustained gender dysphoria to flourish in their lifetime—in the strongly gendered society in which they happen to find themselves, with the resources now available, rather than in some theoretical or future universe—demands that society facilitate a social and possibly a physical transition.[16]

To be sure, a community's embrace of a nonbinary identity or a gender transition does not solve all problems or relieve all suffering. Rather, it honors nonbinary and trans* persons' finitude by returning them on their terms to the still particular, local networks that support a robust life of practical interdependence and mutual indwelling. In addition, it honors other community members' finitude by insisting that their own needs for interdependence trump their isolating discomfort with the unfamiliar. In the future, might long-range justice work yield visions of gender that dissolve such conflicts? Perhaps. But respect for mortal finitude dictates that we prefer the most robust solution that is possible now, a solution that inevitably reiterates our society's current understandings of gender even as it riffs on them transformatively.

Attentive listening, expansion and fortification of interdependence, and concern for the urgency of mortality should be uncontroversial. Yet, lawmakers in multiple states have acted to restrict participation and/or care without attending to trans* and nonbinary people or their parents and without offering viable alternative pathways to flourishing. According to the Trans Legislation Tracker, at last count, anti-trans* bills of some kind have been introduced in all states except Delaware.[17] The United States Conference of Catholic Bishops has also made binding statements, without evidence of having consulted widely with trans* and nonbinary people themselves.[18] This is epistemological presumption: not just a failure of humility and compassionate curiosity, but a fundamental revulsion to new information. It contradicts trans* and nonbinary people's experience of their own finite, complex, and wonderful spirit-flesh. It flattens the mystery of our spirit-flesh creation. It leads to the denial of resources that trans* and nonbinary people have decided upon after long discernment in their interdependent networks of support, including family, friends, doctors, and counselors. And because trans* and nonbinary people come along with a multitude of relationships, this attitude wounds not just them but the whole interdependent network of which each is a part. In our ignorance, we cannot afford such a presumption; and in our mortal finitude, we cannot afford such a loss.

But an ethical mandate without action changes nothing in the finite, urgent present. Here womanist virtues of sometimes playful resistance come into play. Library drag story hours invest in future interdependence by widening the diversity of young children's everyday, local communities. Catholic schools' public refusal to embrace anti-LGBTQ+ diocesan policies strengthens their fabrics of interdependence and increases LGBTQ+ students' trust and confidence that they can safely contribute to their communities.[19] In both cases resistance transforms traditions by using those traditions' own pathways.

FLOURISHING AMID FAILURE, GRIEF, AND REGRET

Pregnancy is morally fraught because so much is at stake: it is our only pathway to birth, and only the female-bodied among us can become pregnant, two facts that can be at odds when we focus on finitude and interdependence. Protecting bodily integrity and the right to manage one's own body in the context of one's particular social connections, which as we saw is essential to thinking clearly about gender, must also be an element of any moral argument about conception or preventing it, or about pregnancy, abortion, or birth. But to whom do those rights belong? And are rights the end of the story?

Our discussion of gender suggests that rights are only one element of an ethic of pregnancy. In any case, they have not settled the issue for Christians. For instance, Margaret Kamitsuka has forthrightly argued that theology affirms both women's autonomy and fetuses' human status: even though a fetus is human and has value, a pregnant woman's autonomy supersedes a human fetus's right to life, giving her the moral right to abort it or to continue her pregnancy at any point.[20] On the other hand, most Catholic pro-life arguments insist that from the moment of fertilization, an embryonic human's right to life trumps rights to health, safety, and autonomy for the woman in whose body they reside and are sustained, because these rank below life itself in the hierarchy of goods. Or, in an intermediate mode, if the weight of the right shifts from woman to embryo or fetus during pregnancy, when and why does it shift, and what are the moral implications? These debates have been stuck at an impasse for more than fifty years. Rights arguments will not solve them. Finitude does not solve them either, but it interjects an important framework: if we begin with particularity, finitude, and mortality, our energy will shift from debating reproductive rights to strengthening our networks of interdependence, at all levels, in order to promote flourishing here and now.

Liberationist feminist ethics, like many Roman Catholic social justice arguments born of the social encyclicals, sometimes imply that there would be no hard moral choices in a perfectly just world because people's goods would not conflict, and we would have adequate resources. Yet, as Sandra Sullivan-Dunbar and Jeannine Hill Fletcher argue so eloquently, caring for ourselves and others who rely on us with scarce resources and limited amounts of energy is a fact of our finite existence, not a product of sin. Just as finitude reminds us that a perfectly just world would entail pain and suffering, it implies that such a world would also generate genuine moral dilemmas. Some of them would be tragic dilemmas: situations in which needs that we are immediately responsible to meet are in conflict, and there is no way to satisfy one without harming someone by failing to fulfill the other.[21] There would still be days on which the sum of others' need came to more than the amount we could humanly give, even with the support our available networks provided. On a larger scale, the defeat of sin and the advent of justice would not be the end of earthquakes, or hurricanes, or forest fires, or illnesses of mind and body. Although without the sin of climate abuse these disasters might have befallen us less frequently and have been less severe, they would still have occurred, and our finitude would sometimes have produced tragic dilemmas as a result. The end of sin is not the end of human, embodied need and human, embodied finitude, and so it is not the beginning of a perfect match between need and resource in every place, in every moment.

Decisions need not rise to the level of tragedy to demand that we choose for one thing at the cost of deciding against another. People to whom we are linked make claims on us, and our own finitude dictates that we not fulfill some of those claims if we honestly judge that the resources our bodies, time, and networks provide us cannot stretch to cover them without harming the good projects and relationships to which we have already made a commitment. We can and often must refuse.[22] This typically is not a matter of being forced into a tight corner but of (usually uncontroversially) planning one's vocation around one's own mortality, energy, and situation. Committing to care for an intellectually disabled relative might mean rejecting on-call professions like medicine or plumbing for work that can be performed within the available hours of adult daycare. One justification for celibate vocations is freeing oneself from ties that would restrict one's response to a multitude of other people's needs.

Taking on pregnancy and parenthood demands similar either/or decisions. We say that Mary's yes to the angel of God (Luke 1:26–38) was free, by which we mean that she consciously accepted one finite pathway—pregnancy, along with the task and identity of the Mother of God—and rejected other viable callings. The tradition of the Immaculate Conception interprets Mary's decision as virtually predetermined, given that it holds that she was chosen for the task before her birth. But if Mary was truly a finite human, no matter how saintly, she made a free choice. Scripture is silent on the question of how many people may have freely, responsibly refused pregnancy and the (universally indispensable) role of Mother of God in favor of another genuine vocation before Mary accepted it. Would a contemporary Mary have said yes if she already had five children, or if she were a wildland firefighter who was asked at the beginning of the summer?

Experientially, this necessary freedom in response to finitude becomes less matter-of-fact when it entails turning away from someone to whom we are linked, actively choosing against their need, possibly leaving it unfulfilled in order to meet another's, or even our own. For instance, if our elderly parents live far apart, moving close by to assist one means choosing to be less accessible to the other. We must face not only our parent's genuine disappointment and possible harm but our own distress at the damage and disappointment they suffer, our grief at our unavoidable refusal to fulfill our interdependent connection to them, and our regret that in fulfilling one person's need, another's has gone at least partly unanswered. The more closely connected to a person we are, the more these decisions feel like betrayals.[23] This could be the case even if the distant parent had nonfamily support: they still would not have *our* care. Such decisions may yield relational fractures and unmet needs, both of which are failures of interdependent relationship. How can we, and the one from whom we have turned away, flourish despite this brutal consequence of created finitude?

Traditional Catholic moral reasoning proposes one answer. It reminds us that our decision to care more intensively for one parent than the other is at least not wrong. Because sin is always a matter of free choice, it must be possible for us to avoid sin when we are faced with two mutually exclusive claims; there must be at least one morally good choice. We are expected to fulfill the need that is weightier or that obligates us more—hence the Vatican position on abortion, in which the good of life itself trumps every life-dependent good—or, if they are equally compelling, we can choose. Our practical failure to meet the other need is not a moral failure, but a product of our finitude, and thus it is not a sin, and no one—including the person from whom we have turned away—can justly blame us.

Yet, like an analysis based solely on rights, this approach is at best a first step. First and most importantly, it does not address the unmet need. Second, it does not take up our entanglement in disappointment, abandonment, fracture, and even betrayal—whether we are the ones who have failed to respond to everyone who needs us or the ones who have been left unaided. Third, an ethic that prioritizes avoiding sin over pursuing the good and holy runs against the principle of *theosis*, of growing into the likeness of God. Simply declaring such failures non-sins implies that we should dust off our hands, or others', and forget; instead, we must figure out how to incorporate both failure and grief into our growth in and toward the divine.

Our first step is simple acceptance. Because we are created as mortal persons, not superheroes, even in an ideal world we would frequently make such mutually exclusive, free decisions, and we would often suffer from others' free, good decisions to turn away from our needs and desires. Even in an ideal world, we would not be able to make up for all of today's unmet needs and hopes tomorrow. We must be gentle with ourselves in this respect.

If we end here, however, we simply exonerate ourselves and one another without acknowledging the intensifying unmet needs and disappointed hopes that result from such decisions. Our second step is to accept that even in a sinless world, we would be ineffectual without robust, self-consciously collaborative networks of interdependence. This is the communal, trinitarian side of *theosis*: God became human so that humans could together become God.[24] If serving as a nearby resource for one of my parents means that I cannot do so for the other, I can gather those close to me (including my parents, who surely should have a say) to find a solution, and my brother, or my cousin, or a good family friend—or all three—can step up. As Mary Jo Iozzio pointed out, social service nonprofits and government agencies are also indispensable elements of our support system. There is no going it alone; we must construct and maintain dynamic networks of interdependence.

Perhaps unexpectedly, robust networks not only meet existing needs but also reinforce themselves by encouraging us to have faith in them. As Haker argues, consistent structures of support create an experience of security that allows us to take good risks when making hard choices, because they lessen our anxious insistence on making an absolutely comprehensive accounting of needs and resources before pledging ourselves to something. We might not commit to anything or anyone if we had to undertake this daunting audit, and if we believed that abandonment was likely. For example, scripture tells us that over time Mary the Mother of God drew on further angelic intervention; her husband, Joseph (Matt 1:18–25); her cousin Elizabeth (Luke 1:39–45); a stable keeper (Luke 2:7); the disciple whom Jesus loved (John 19:26–27); and unnamed others about whom she could not possibly have known and on whom she could not possibly have counted before accepting pregnancy and the role of Mother of God.[25] We can imagine that she said "yes" because she had realistic confidence, based in experience, that these networks of interdependence would provide, without needing to know exactly how. The contrasting story is the one of Hagar, who was forced to become a surrogate mother, who was cut off from networks of interdependence, who was handed the tragic dilemma of abusive enslavement or deadly wilderness, and who concluded reasonably that her involuntary motherhood was about to lead to her own and her child's death (Gen 21:8–21).[26] The only rational response to her abandonment was despair.

We would need networks of interdependence in order to flourish even in a sinless world, and even (as Lisa Powell argues) in heaven. But as Hagar's story reminds us, we do not inhabit a sinless world. Social injustice is responsible for a high percentage of our tragic dilemmas. A classic example comes from *Sophie's Choice*, William Styron's novel about a young woman whom Nazi soldiers force to choose to save either her daughter or her son, knowing that they will kill the other.[27] Most of the caretaking dilemmas that Sullivan-Dunbar and Hill Fletcher describe arise in part from social injustice, too: being unjustly deprived of the time and resources to attend to people in our care with the focus and energy they deserve, or being unjustly tasked with the care of too many. Too often we are torn between caring poorly for too many and failing to care for some at all.

Although not all pregnancy dilemmas arise from injustice, it plays a large role in many of them. Many decisions about pregnancy come down to this question: with the finite resources and networks that I can count on, can I care for myself, all the people for whom I must already care, and another child? Gross social injustices mean that the honest answer to this last question is often "no." The Turnaway Study[28]—which compared the family outcomes for low-income women who received and were denied abortions—confirmed this: the women who gave birth were less able to support their families financially and less likely to leave abusive partners than women who received abortions, and their children also did less well developmentally. Society bears the blame for creating a tragic dilemma in which a woman—unjustly sidelined from both the structural and the informal networks of interdependence that flourishing in finitude requires—lacks the resources to say yes to a pregnancy without harming herself and her existing children.[29]

Anti-abortion law exacerbates this problem by further isolating women from the very networks that support them. By threatening legal action, current U.S. laws that criminalize abortion drive women into closets of secrecy.[30] In this way they additionally fracture women's already fragmented networks of interdependence—networks that, if strengthened instead of weakened, would give women with healthy pregnancies true freedom to decide their paths, and women with nonviable pregnancies the support to mourn their losses, without fear of prosecution—not to mention the security of knowing that a condition that threatens their lives will be treated promptly and safely.

The importance of access to resources and networks of support is part of the argument women of color make for reproductive justice. Without robust, reliable networks of interdependence—accessible through well-resourced structural necessities such as affordable nearby childcare, adequate wages at a job with a short commute, and reasonable rent in a stable community, along with high-bandwidth informal networks of interdependence—women cannot make free choices about parenthood because they cannot be confident of meeting their own needs, let alone the needs of those closest to them.[31] Thus reproductive justice advocates are in a fight for a right that is more foundational, practically, than any of the other rights involved in the debates over abortion and pregnancy: the right to networks of interdependence that allow women to choose to carry a pregnancy, give birth, and parent safely and well. From the perspective of finitude, interdependent, well-resourced community is the precondition for considering what it might mean to fulfill fetuses' right to life and women's right to self-determination.

Thus, beginning with created finitude reshapes a feminist, Christian ethic around pregnancy in two ways. First, its foundational moral imperative must be supporting robust, dynamic, well-resourced networks of interdependency from the most local and informal through the governmental to the international level. Second, even were this effort to succeed, it would not wipe out dilemmas, including dilemmas around pregnancy, entirely. And this fact leads us to the third step in accepting the consequences of our finitude, which is a matter of the spirit.

Finitude is a created, embodied, temporal, joyous good. It is also wrenching, even in the best case. As

Bryan Massingale, Emilie Townes, and Kate Jackson-Meyer write, practical action in response to inescapable suffering cannot erase our distress at it.[32] Our wounded spirits need lament, which works on us at a level deeper, Massingale says, than the "discursive or intellectual."[33] Together, in community before God, we can help one another to name sorrows and wounds that would remain unlabeled and uncomforted otherwise; take the time, space, and companionship to mourn; and image the suffering of the Trinity in grief and pain over the passion. Lament throws us back on the mystery of God's grace, generating faith and hope amid the ashes, faith and hope that renew our energy for the justice work that we can undertake. This is exactly the kind of communal grieving and support that Sophie, the character in Styron's novel, did not have or seek after her cruel treatment by Nazi guards, with disastrous consequences for her postwar life.

For Townes, communal lament is a response of protest and hope specifically against the unjust, ongoing suffering we endure at the hands of other humans, seemingly with God's permission; for Massingale, lament is especially about the historically white Catholic theological academy's confession of its own moral failure to render race visible in ethics and theology. Kate Jackson-Meyer proposes that we lament not just the harm we suffer, and the culpable harm we do, but also the harm that comes to others through us thanks to the dilemmas that both injustice and plain finitude impose on us, as well as the anguish we suffer at having failed to fulfill others' real needs.[34] This communal practice, she suggests, could bind us together against the temptation to blame each other for failures that arise from our common finitude. Communal compassion in the form of hopeful lament turns out to be essential not only to our flourishing amid intractable injustices but also to our flourishing together within our finitude, which serves up tragedy even in the absence of injustice.

However, lament must not be a shortcut around hardnosed, communal self-examination of our own complicity in injustice. Private lament of our own inability to meet others' needs invites solipsism. After all, the original impetus of liberation theology was grief over Christians' oppression of their siblings in Christ, in the name of Christ. In addition, Townes specifically recommends lament as a Black response to racism. Lament of the failures that our good, created finitude inevitably entails must take place within the largest, most diverse possible community of interdependence if it is not to reinforce injustice in the name of embracing our finitude.

Thus, with respect to pregnancy, finitude reminds us that tragic dilemmas are unavoidable. Our moral mandate is to remove the unnecessary ones, not by developing ever finer moral distinctions but by working to reduce injustice and strengthen our structural and informal networks of interdependence at every level, ensuring that everyone has confident access to the support they need to make truly free choices about pregnancy. Our spiritual mandate is to create communal traditions of mourning and lamentation for the losses we cannot avoid, the people we cannot aid, and the pathways we cannot pursue—whether as a consequence of injustice or as a corollary of our finitude.

Together, these ruminations on gender and pregnancy also remind us that epistemic humility comes in two kinds: alongside modesty before our own practical, temporal, finite knowledge, we must be humble before the mystery of our gendered social lives and our reproductively sexed creation. Our gendered identities are fungible, but our bodies are so only to a point: the immediate risks, joys, and catastrophes of pregnancy and birth belong only to the female-bodied, a fact for which both social systems and informal networks of interdependence must account. Still, flattening gender and reproductive sex into an equivalence reduces the mystery of our divine creation to a formula, oversimplifying the image of God that we reflect. This is idolatry.

CONCLUSION

The word *flourishing* has appeared endlessly in the foregoing chapters, making the argument feel a bit circular. As this conclusion will make clear, defining it conclusively is an eschatological project. Still, we are closer to a description. Beginning ethics with the goodness of our created finitude reveals how limited and unrealistic the assumptions underlying Christian visions of a good life can be. Bodily perfection turns out to be culturally specific and exclusive; perfect health is elusive; social norms—gender, for example—can be arbitrary and unjust; ideals of egalitarian mutuality rely on an eventual equality that may not come to pass; perfect virtue and perfect moral aims either are artificially narrow, encourage an anti-body dualism, or turn out to be impossible in the messiness of even a sinless world. Instead, finitude remakes virtue and our view of the good life, leading us to a rich vision of universal interdependence that depends on differences of personality, body, skill, and capacity—a vision that gathers up health and illness, ability and disability, healing and injury, and birth and death into a dynamic, unending process of attentive, humble mutual support among mortal, spirit-fleshed people.

To flourish in finitude is simply to live in and savor the unfancy, embodied dailiness of eating well, wearing clothes that make us feel good, spending our time meaningfully, and going home to a supportive household or a robust cohort of friends who multiply our joys and divide our griefs. To flourish in finitude is to live within a resilient network of interdependence in which we help each other bear what we cannot solve, enabling each other to trust that we will have support when we take risks for the good: bearing and raising children, for instance, but also coming out and living out as LGBTQ+ people, taking public stances for causes we believe in, committing to each other in lifelong partnership, pursuing vocations, and so many more pledges that require robust frameworks of support at every level from the most intimate to the most institutional. Even in a sinless world, it would mean gathering to lament the losses and disappointments we cannot help suffering and the tragic decisions we cannot help making even with others' support, holding each other into hope. In the world we know, it also means joining together to lament the injustices we suffer and collaborating to resist and eradicate them creatively. Our first test of any norm or practice is whether it strengthens this network or weakens it.

Starting with finitude also leads through interdependence straight to the demand for justice. A network of interdependence that can absorb illness, or death, or disaster demands time, energy, resources, and security enough to maintain it. Thus, as with care, flourishing demands right relations, adequate and fairly distributed resources, protection from attack, and work that leaves us the temporal and financial elasticity to turn to others or to the community when called. The surest damper to justice is a situation that forces people to spend all their time and energy simply on surviving.

As we have seen, this view of finite, just flourishing has implications for theology, for method in ethics, and for our idea of vocation. In theology, flourishing in finitude scuttles the ideas that the discipline of ethics is about perfect reasoning and the practice of ethics, about perfect virtue, perfect adherence to unchanging rules, or perfect results. Better said, it scuttles the idea that perfection is the end point of a long process of refining reasoning or purging flaws until only shining, static purity remains. Not only does this suggest that perfection is the result of cutting away rather than building up, but the moment we begin to define perfection—whether it is bodily, relational, rational, or structural—we invariably import arbitrary, exclusionary norms.[1] What does a perfect nose look like, for example? What is a perfect family? What is perfect reason (and what of those who cannot practice it)?

Beginning ethics with finite flourishing tells us that perfection is dynamism, not stasis, because it is continuous, ever more responsive interchange within shifting relations of interdependence amid people with diverse needs and abilities. This view of perfection—as an ever-improving process rather than a final state—fits well with an "ontology of becoming" that honors our bodies—bodies that, as Robyn Henderson-Espinoza says, are "always becoming and always becoming different from [themselves]."[2] It also coheres with *theosis* as communal growing-into-God. If this is so, Powell proposes, perhaps the perfection of resurrected life, too, is not static but dynamic: "Maybe...we become increasingly intertwined, thus more defined by our relationships with God and each other, more transparent in our need, more vulnerable, more eager to meet the needs of another, and ever replenished."[3] Perfection is not an end point but an eternal process of growing into the image of the Trinity, with its ever-shifting relations of generous and needy interdependence and mutual indwelling.

Beginning with finitude affects ethics methodologically as well. Stressing relational processes of listening over deductive determination of permanent norms, an ethic of finitude rejects what Pope Francis has called "a climate of closure" for a stance of epistemic humility and openness to change. Because "our understanding of the human person changes with time, and our consciousness also deepens," he says, ethicists must "take the risk of making changes" that "[develop] from the roots upward."[4] It is not as if people at the roots have not been speaking. Rather, ethicists need to attend to what is already clearly audible and invite what has not been safe to say aloud—particularly at intersections of oppression or from people who have no public voice.

Finally, finitude is about vocation-in-interdependence. In our daily lives, flourishing and caring must happen within finite boundaries. We have only sixteen or seventeen waking hours each day, many of which we must use to care for ourselves. As one friend pointed out, our energy is limited, too. We must set priorities: How will we decide what we will do with our finite energy and time? As another pointed out, our attention is possibly our most precious resource, because we cannot multitask, we cannot truly concentrate on more than one task—or person—at a time.[5] To what and to whom will we attend? Our location and era are finite too. What sort of life do we choose here and now? What does it mean, as William Werpehowski writes, to be "summoned in one's own history before God" "in [our] specific time, place, and relationships"?[6] Or as Daniel Horan says, to be [called] in "our utter particularity and individual identity"?[7] Or as Nancy Pineda Madrid says, to respond to our community's call?[8] Our lives are not our own; we must take up a sliver of the project of concrete interdependence in our place and time, in faith and confidence in others' collaboration, and in full knowledge that the going will not be easy.

This brings us back to Jesus incarnate. We image a humanly finite Jesus Christ whose own tragic dilemma—stay here, work signs, and preach, or go home and tend to Lazarus—led to his friend's death; who called out Roman oppression but did not topple it, and but for it would possibly have lived long and—as a man—have died of prostate cancer or heart disease, like everyone else; who animated and was sustained by an enormous network of support, only a few of whose names we know. In his divinity, he raised Lazarus; in his divinity, he rose; but his wounded rising confirms the inseparability of his divinity and his humanity, reminding us that even in the best circumstances we must flourish within the bounds of woundedness and mortality. We can image and grow into God only as embodied, finite people.

It brings us back to the Trinity, the ethical and existential communion of love among multiple persons who indwell each other interdependently and dynamically. We cannot think of any without thinking of all, just as we cannot think of a human person without all the others in their dynamic network of interdependence. We can image—and through *theosis* grow into—the Trinity not individually but only in interdependent community.

And it brings us back to the saints, for whom complete devotion to God and earnest desire for perfection coexisted with doing what they could within constrained circumstances, and inspiring others to do the same. In contradiction to the old hymn, they never "from their labors rest" but, providentially for us, fulfill interdependence by crossing time and space to comfort us in our laments and strengthen our efforts at listening, compassion, and justice.[9] Their lives collectively remind us that flourishing is embodied, messy, interdependent, tragic, joyful, always a work in progress—and our common calling. Like them, we can image and grow into God only in a collaborative trial-and-error effort inspired by devotion, compassion, attentiveness, and justice.

NOTES

INTRODUCTION

1. On the futility of commercial approaches, see Pooja Lakshmin, *Real Self-Care: A Transformative Program for Redefining Wellness (Crystals, Cleanses, and Bubble Baths Not Included)* (New York: Penguin, 2023).

2. According to the Pew Research Center, the U.S. gender pay gap persists: in 2022, women's average earnings totaled 82 percent of men's. Rakesh Kochhar, "The Enduring Grip of the Gender Pay Gap," Pew Research Center, March 1, 2023, https://www.pewresearch.org/social-trends/2023/03/01/the-enduring-grip-of-the-gender-pay-gap/.

3. Carol P. Christ and Judith Plaskow, eds., *Womanspirit Rising: A Feminist Reader in Religion*, Harper Forum Books (San Francisco: Harper & Row, 1979), 19–52. Mary Daly, *Amazon Grace: Re-calling the Courage to Sin Big* (New York: Palgrave Macmillan, 2006). Carter Heyward, *Touching Our Strength: The Erotic as Power and the Love of God* (San Francisco: Harper & Row, 1989). Rita Nakashima Brock, *Journeys by Heart: A Christology of Erotic Power* (Eugene, OR: Wipf & Stock, 2008).

4. In later chapters, all woman-affirming theologies are included under the shorthand "feminist" unless specified

otherwise. The intention is not to erode the important, literally critical differences among them but to consider what else may be shared by approaches that intersect in a Venn diagram with the flourishing of women-identified people at the center.

5. Elizabeth A. Johnson, *Ask the Beasts: Darwin and the God of Love* (London: Bloomsbury, 2014), 219.

I. FEMINIST THEOLOGIES ON FINITUDE

1. Rosemary Radford Ruether, "What Is Feminism?," *Feminism and Religion*, August 7, 2023, https://feminismandreligion.com/rosemary-radford-ruether-on-feminism/.

2. Carol P. Christ and Judith Plaskow, eds., *Womanspirit Rising: A Feminist Reader in Religion* (San Francisco: Harper & Row, 1979); Judith Plaskow and Carol P. Christ, eds., *Weaving the Visions: New Patterns in Feminist Spirituality* (San Francisco: Harper & Row, 1989). Christ and Plaskow expressed their equality by reversing the order in which their names appeared as editors in the second book.

3. An important later text in this regard is Elizabeth A. Johnson, CSJ, *She Who Is: The Mystery of God in Feminist Theological Discourse* (New York: Crossroad, 1992), 155.

4. Nelle Morton, "The Goddess as Metaphoric Image," in Plaskow and Christ, *Weaving the Visions*, 211–18.

5. Rosemary Radford Ruether, *Sexism and God-Talk: Toward a Feminist Theology* (Boston: Beacon Press, 1983), 109–14.

6. Sarah Lucia Hoagland, *Lesbian Ethics: Toward New Value* (Palo Alto: Institute of Lesbian Studies, 1989), 54–68.

7. The pun is a reference to Boston Women's Health Collective, *Our Bodies, Ourselves: A Book by and for Women* (Boston: Boston Women's Health Collective, 1971).

8. Many Latina feminist theologians prefer *Latina* to *mujerista*.

9. Intersectionality is a matter not of complex identity but of complex, interacting oppressions. For the original theorization of intersectionality, see Kimberle Crenshaw, "Mapping the Margins: Intersectionality, Identity Politics, and Violence against Women of Color," *Stanford Law Review* 43, no. 6 (1991): 1241–99.

10. For a similar concept in womanist theology, see Emilie M. Townes's theorization of everydayness in *Womanist Ethics and the Cultural Production of Evil* (New York: Palgrave, 2006), 159–65.

11. Carmen Nanko-Fernández, "Lo Cotidiano as Locus Theologicus," in *The Wiley Blackwell Companion to Latino/a Theology*, ed. Orlando Espín (Malden, MA: Wiley-Blackwell, 2015), 13–33, at 21.

12. Nancy Pineda-Madrid, "Feminist Theory and Latina Feminist/Mujerista Theologizing," in Espín, *The Wiley Blackwell Companion to Latino/a Theology*, 348–63, at 351.

13. Audre Lorde, "The Master's Tools Will Never Dismantle the Master's House," in *Sister Outsider: Essays and Speeches* (Berkeley, CA: Crossing Press, 1984), 110–13.

14. Katie Geneva Cannon, "Hitting a Straight Lick with a Crooked Stick: The Womanist Dilemma in the Development of a Black Liberation Ethic," *The Annual of the Society of Christian Ethics* (1987): 165–77, at 166.

15. Katie Geneva Cannon, *Black Womanist Ethics* (Atlanta: Scholars Press, 1988).

16. Emilie M. Townes, *Womanist Ethics and the Cultural Production of Evil* (New York: Palgrave Macmillan, 2006), 61–62. Townes's strategy resonates with Ada María Isasi-Díaz's concept *burlando al opresor*. See Ada María Isasi-Díaz, "Burlando

al Opresor: Mocking/Tricking the Oppressor; Dreams and Hopes of Hispanas/Latinas and Mujeristas," *Theological Studies* 65, no 2 (2004): 340–63.

17. On creativity under constraint, see Jeannine Hill Fletcher, *Motherhood as Metaphor: Engendering Interreligious Dialogue* (New York: Fordham University Press, 2013), chap. 4, 197, 209.

18. One important exception is Emilie Townes's 1998 work, *Breaking the Fine Rain of Death*, which focuses on systemic healthcare injustice that results in disproportionate Black illness, suffering, and death; endorses lament as the beginning of a response to this indignity and evil; and recommends asset-based strategies to counter this injustice and strengthen community. See Emilie M. Townes, *Breaking the Fine Rain of Death: African-American Health Issues and a Womanist Ethic of Care* (New York: Continuum, 1998).

19. John Paul II, *Man and Woman He Created Them: A Theology of the Body*, trans. Michael Waldstein, new trans. based on the John Paul II archives (Boston: Pauline Books & Media, 2006).

20. Hille Haker, "Vulnerable Agency: Human Dignity and Gendered Violence," in *Towards a Critical Political Ethics: Catholic Ethics and Social Challenges* (Basel: Schwabe Verlag, 2020), 135–67, at 139.

21. Haker, "Vulnerable Agency," 140. See Judith Butler, "Precarious Life, Vulnerability, and the Ethics of Cohabitation," *The Journal of Speculative Philosophy* 26, no. 2 (2012): 134–51. For more on the distinction between Butler's approach and an already, always morally normative understanding of essential vulnerability, see Danielle Petherbridge, "What's Critical about Vulnerability? Rethinking Interdependence, Recognition, and Power," *Hypatia* 31, no. 3 (2016): 589–604.

Both Haker and Petherbridge draw on Axel Honneth, "Integrity and Disrespect: Principles of a Conception of Morality Based on a Theory of Recognition," in *The Fragmented World of the Social: Essays in Social and Political Philosophy*, ed. Charles W. Wright (Albany: SUNY Press, 1995), 247–60.

22. See Haker, "Vulnerable Agency, 159–64. See also Alisa L. Carse, "Vulnerability, Integrity, and Human Flourishing," in *Health and Human Flourishing: Religion, Medicine, and Moral Anthropology*, ed. Carol Taylor, CFSN, and Roberto Dell'Oro (Washington, DC: Georgetown University Press, 2006), 33–52.

23. Rita Dove, "Unaccompanied Anthem," The Poetry Foundation, August 28, 2023, https://www.poetryfoundation.org/poetrymagazine/poems/159786/unaccompanied-anthem.

24. See Daniel P. Horan, OFM, *Catholicity and Emerging Personhood: A Contemporary Theological Anthropology* (Maryknoll, NY: Orbis, 2019), 135: "What makes an individual an individual according to Scotus's principle of individuation (*entitas individualis* or *haecceitas*) is identical with a thing's very existence or being."

25. Emma Samman, Elizabeth Presler-Marshall, and Nicola Jones, with Tanvi Bhatkal, Claire Melamed, Maria Stavropoulou, and John Wallace, "Women's Work: Mothers, Children, and the Global Childcare Crisis" (London: Overseas Development Institute, 2016), 9. https://bettercarenetwork.org/sites/default/files/Women's%20work-%20Mothers%2C%20children%20and%20the%20global%20childcare%20crisis.pdf.

26. Samman et al., "Women's Work," 9.

27. Sandra Sullivan-Dunbar, *Human Dependency and Christian Ethics* (Cambridge: Cambridge University Press, 2015), 220. See 194, 223–30.

28. Sullivan-Dunbar, *Human Dependency*, 1–26.

29. See Sharon V. Betcher, "Bearing the Brunt of Corporeality: Hope for Souls and Societies Begins with the Embrace of Fragile Flesh and Bodies in Pain," *Sojourners Magazine* 50, no. 5 (May 2021): 22–27; Sharon V. Betcher, "The Picture of Health: 'Nature' at the Intersection of Disability, Religion and Ecology," *Worldviews* 19, no. 1 (2015): 9–33, doi:10.1163/15685357-01901002; Doreen Freeman, "A Feminist Theology of Disability," *Feminist Theology* 29 (January 2002): 71–85; Monique Nicole Moultrie, "'In the World to Come God Will Sign': Challenges to Feminist Theologies of Embodiment and Wholeness and a Model of Inclusivity for Persons with Disabilities," *Journal of Religion, Disability & Health* 11, no. 1 (2007): 27–36; and Meredith Minister, "Religion and (Dis)Ability in Early Feminism," *Journal of Feminist Studies in Religion* 29, no. 2 (Fall 2013): 5–24. Founding mother of feminist disability theology Nancy Eiesland embraced the liberationist approach but rejected the idea that resurrected bodies are physically perfect. See Nancy L. Eiesland, *The Disabled God: Toward a Liberatory Theology of Disability* (Nashville: Abingdon Press, 1994).

30. See, for example, Deborah Beth Creamer, *Disability and Christian Theology: Embodied Limits and Constructive Possibilities* (New York: Oxford, 2009), 107.

31. Jana Marguerite Bennett, "Being 'Stuck' between Stanley and the Feminists (the Proverbial Rock and a Hard Place)," in *Unsettling Arguments: A Festschrift on the Occasion of Stanley Hauerwas's 70th Birthday*, ed. Charles R. Pinches, Kelly S. Robinson, and Charles M. Collier (Eugene, OR: Cascade Books, 2010), 229–45, at 245.

32. See Mayra Rivera Rivera, "Thinking Bodies: The Spirit of a Latina Incarnational Imagination," in *Decolo-*

nizing Epistemologies: Latina/o Theology and Philosophy, ed. Ada-María Isasi-Díaz and Eduardo Mendieta (New York: Fordham University Press, 2011), 207–25, at 212.

33. Katarzyna Galasinska and Aleksandra Szymkow, "The More Fertile, the More Creative: Changes in Women's Creative Potential across the Ovulatory Cycle," *International Journal of Environmental Research and Public Health* 18, no. 10 (2021): 5390, doi: 10.3390/ijerph18105390.

34. Deborah Beth Creamer, "Disability Theology," *Religion Compass* 6, no. 7 (July 2012): 339–46, at 341 and 343. See also Nancy Mairs, "Growing into God," *Journal of Feminist Studies in Religion* 26, no. 2 (Fall 2010): 137–39; and Elizabeth Stuart, "Disruptive Bodies: Disability, Embodiment and Sexuality," in *The Good News of the Body: Sexual Theology and Feminism*, ed. Lisa Isherwood (New York: NYU Press, 2000), 166–84. Stuart points out that labels are limiting in a restrictive sense, given that our fundamental identity is our baptismal identity. See Elisabeth Stuart, "Sacramental Flesh," in *Queer Theology: Rethinking the Western Body*, ed. Gerard Loughlin (Malden, MA: Blackwell, 2007), 65–75. Sullivan-Dunbar also writes that "our agency is shaped by our limits" (*Human Dependency*, 227). See also Thomas E. Reynolds, "The Cult of Normalcy," *Christian Reflection* 45 (2012): 25–33; thanks to Kyle Stevenson for this reference.

35. Creamer, *Disability and Christian Theology*, 96.

36. Creamer, *Disability and Christian Theology*, 103.

37. The Vision Council, "Organizational Overview," August 14, 2023. https://thevisioncouncil.org/sites/default/files/assets/media/TVC_OrgOverview_sheet_2021.pdf.

38. Creamer, *Disability and Christian Theology*, 93–95.

39. Deborah Beth Creamer, "Embracing Limits, Queering Embodiment: Creating/Creative Possibilities for Disability

Theology," *Journal of Feminist Studies in Religion* 26, no. 2 (Fall 2010): 123–27 at 125. Italics added.

40. Creamer, *Disability and Christian Theology*, 102–3, italics added. See also Susan Windley-Daoust, "Is There a 'Theology of the Disabled Body'? John Paul II's Theology of the Body on Limit and Sign," *Journal of Disability and Religion* 20, no. 3 (2016): 163–77, discussed in chapter 2.

41. Creamer occasionally waffles on whether all limits are good or neutral; she implies that some are bad or evil (see *Disability and Christian Theology*, 109, 112, for example). She also does not distinguish among the causes of the limits. Limits that arise from injustice—for instance, disabling lung disease resulting from inadequate safety precautions in mines or chemical plants—are evil. In addition, social circumstances—such as inaccessible public transportation—can turn a limit into a disability.

42. Creamer, *Disability and Christian Theology*, 110.

43. Eiesland, *The Disabled God*, 95–96.

44. Rivera, "Thinking Bodies," 223.

45. Rivera, "Thinking Bodies," 218.

46. Margaret A. Farley, *Changing the Questions: Explorations in Christian Ethics*, ed. Jamie L. Manson (Maryknoll, NY: Orbis, 2015), 269.

47. Sullivan-Dunbar, *Human Dependency*, 211.

II. INTERDEPENDENCE

1. For other theological routes around this conundrum, see John Berkman, "Are Persons with Profound Intellectual Disabilities Sacramental Icons of Heavenly Life? Aquinas on Impairment," *Studies in Christian Ethics* 26, no. 1 (2013): 83–96, and Erinn Staley, "Intellectual Disability and

Mystical Unknowing: Contemporary Insights from Medieval Sources," *Modern Theology* 28, no. 3 (2012): 385–401.

2. Daniel P. Horan, OFM, *Catholicity and Emerging Personhood: A Contemporary Theological Anthropology* (Maryknoll, NY: Orbis, 2019), 37.

3. Susan A. Ross, *Anthropology: Seeking Light and Beauty* (Collegeville, MN: Liturgical Press, 2012), 155–62.

4. M. Shawn Copeland, *Enfleshing Freedom: Body, Race, and Being* (Minneapolis: Fortress Press, 2010), 24.

5. Hannah Bacon, "*Thinking* the Trinity as Resource for Feminist Theology Today?," *Crosscurrents* (December 2012): 444–64, at 456; Lisa D. Powell, *The Disabled God Revisited: Trinity, Christology, and Liberation* (London: T&T Clark, 2023), 53, 41.

6. Sara Butler, "Feminist Christology: A New Iconoclasm?," *The Thomist* 83 (2019): 493–519, at 506–7.

7. These unknown particularities—what we might call identities—are elements of what Elizabeth Johnson calls a "multipolar" anthropology. See Elizabeth A. Johnson, CSJ, *She Who Is: The Mystery of God in Feminist Theological Discourse* (New York: Crossroad, 1993), 155. Sara Butler argues that Jesus's maleness carries heavier symbolic weight than the other this-but-not-that particular dimensions of his finitude, but this is because she argues that male and female natures are different and complementary. I agree that Jesus was male but not that there is a "male nature" that can be juxtaposed to a "female human nature" and that these two constitute more essential particularities than other dimensions of human being (see Butler, "Feminist Christology," 512–15).

8. Lisa Isherwood, *The Fat Jesus: Christianity and Body Image* (New York: Seabury, 2008).

9. Miguel J. Romero, "The Goodness and Beauty of Our Fragile Flesh: Moral Theologians and Our Engagement With 'Disability,'" *Journal of Moral Theology* 6, Special Issue 2 (2017): 206–53; quotations at 235 and 206. For Thomas, Romero shows, the senses provide the material on which the intellect operates; for instance, a body that can hear (including loud noises), feel (including pain and injury), and so forth is imperative for intellectual growth. I am arguing that while intellect is one way toward God, the finite body provides other pathways as well.

10. Powell argues that in the incarnation God's kenosis, or self-emptying, consists in receiving, taking up, or taking in humanity with all its finite, embodied characteristics (see *The Disabled God Revisited*, for example, 65). I am not convinced that receiving is kenotic.

11. See Margaret A. Farley, *Changing the Questions: Explorations in Christian Ethics*, ed. Jamie L. Manson (Maryknoll, NY: Orbis, 2015), 269; Jeannine Hill Fletcher, *Motherhood as Metaphor: Engendering Interreligious Dialogue* (New York: Fordham University Press, 2013), 211.

12. Mayra Rivera Rivera, "Thinking Bodies: The Spirit of a Latina Incarnational Imagination," in *Decolonizing Epistemologies: Latina/o Theology and Philosophy*, ed. Ada-María Isasi-Díaz and Eduardo Mendieta (New York: Fordham University Press, 2011), 221–23.

13. See also Grace M. Jantzen, *Becoming Divine: Towards a Feminist Philosophy of Religion* (Bloomington: Indiana University Press, 1999) and Luce Irigaray, "Divine Women," in *Women, Knowledge, and Reality: Explorations in Feminist Philosophy*, ed. Ann Garry and Marilyn Pearsall (New York: Routledge, 1996), 471–84. On the connection between incarnation and *theosis*, see, for example, George A. Maloney,

SJ, "Ecumenism and Divinization," *Mid-Stream* 40, nos. 1–2 (Jan.–Apr. 2001): 203–10; Paul L. Gavrilyuk, "The Retrieval of Deification: How a Once-Despised Archaism Became an Ecumenical Desideratum," *Modern Theology* 25, no. 4 (2009): 647–59; and Spyridoula Athanasopoulou-Kypriou, "Icons as Women's Horizon for Their Becoming Divine in the Eastern Orthodox Church: Exploring the Political Dimensions of Iconology and Iconography," *Journal of the European Society of Women in Theological Research* 19 (2011): 67–78.

14. Heleen E. Zorgdrager, "On the Fullness of Salvation: Tracking *Theosis* in Reformed Theology," *Journal of Reformed Theology* 8 (2014): 357–81, at 363; Andrew Louth, *Introducing Eastern Orthodox Theology* (Downers Grove, IL: IVP Academic, 2013), 111.

15. Mark Doox, "Mark Doox," Squarespace (August 7, 2023), https://www.saintsambo.com/work#/our-lady-of-ferguson-missouri-and-all-killed-by-gun-violence/. In the image, Jesus is a potential victim, because he is not yet dead; Doox gives the viewer the option of putting down the gun. In addition, Doox notes that Mary and Jesus Christ raise their hands not in blessing but in response to the "hands up" commands of police and in prayer for God's judgment on the violent. Doox—who also goes by the name "St. Sambo"—calls out racism by giving ironic iconic treatment to racial idolatry: for instance, icons of a Black nanny holding a white Christ child and of a Black man holding a sign that reads "This is not a man." See https://www.saintsambo.com/work. Thanks to Rachel Contos for this reference.

16. Peter's denial can also be interpreted subversively. See Elsie Miranda, "Elsie Miranda Preaches for Palm Sunday," Catholic Women Preach (April 2, 2023), https://www.catholicwomenpreach.org/preaching/04022023.

17. Nancy L. Eiesland, *The Disabled God: Toward a Liberatory Theology of Disability* (Nashville: Abingdon, 1994), 23, 47–48, 98–100, 116.

18. 2 Baruch 50. The book goes on to suggest that once resurrected and recognized, the dead will undergo *some* change—into glory if they are good, and into "torment" and wasting away if they are evil (2 Bar 51). Thanks to Karina Martin Hogan for this reference. See also Rivera, "Thinking Bodies," 221; and 1 Cor 15:35–42. Thanks to Rachel Contos for the latter reference.

19. Copeland, *Enfleshing Freedom*, 83; Powell, *The Disabled God Revisited*, 126. On Thomas Aquinas and our rising in bodies that are "numerically" identical to our earthly ones, see Michael M. Waddell, "Thomas Aquinas and the Resurrection of the (Disabled) Body," *The Saint Anselm Journal* 12, no. 2 (2017): 29–64 at 64.

20. Susan Windley-Daoust, "Is There a 'Theology of the Disabled Body'? John Paul II's Theology of the Body on Limit and Sign," *Journal of Disability and Religion* 20, no. 3 (2016): 163–77, especially 169.

21. Deborah Creamer, *Disability and Christian Theology: Embodied Limits and Constructive Possibilities* (New York: Oxford, 2009), 94–95: "A second and related claim suggests that limits are an *intrinsic* aspect of human existence—part of what it means to be human...each member of the community has a different gift and...it takes all of these differences together to create the body of Christ (1 Corinthians 12)." Sarah Jean Barton, *Becoming the Baptized Body: Disability and the Practice of Christian Community* (Waco, TX: Baylor, 2022). Thanks to Kyle Stevenson for the Barton reference.

22. Hill Fletcher, *Motherhood as Metaphor*, 51, 54, 66. Hill Fletcher does not distinguish unjust limits from others

because in this work she is more interested in their cumulative impact than in their origin. See *Motherhood as Metaphor*, 66 and chapter 4.

23. Sandra Sullivan-Dunbar, *Human Dependency and Christian Ethics* (Cambridge: Cambridge University Press, 2015), 86–94.

24. Susan Abraham, "Praying the Trinity; Transforming Feminist Trinitarian Theologies," *Modern Theology* 30, no. 4 (2014): 582–90, at 590. Windley-Daoust expressly leaves aside John Paul II's gender hierarchy, which is by definition static, to explore the ways in which apparently more and less able members of communities minister to one another dynamically. See also Julie B. Miller, "To Remember Self, to Remember God: Augustine on Sexuality, Relationality, and the Trinity," in *Feminist Interpretations of Augustine*, ed. Judith Chelius Stark (University Park: Pennsylvania State University Press, 2007), 243–79. See also Creamer, *Disability and Christian Theology*, 94–95.

25. Mary Jo Iozzio, "The Writing on the Wall...Alzheimer's Disease: A Daughter's Look at Mom's Faithful Care of Dad," *Journal of Religion, Disability & Health* 9, no. 2 (2005–2006): 49–74, at 55. Iozzio does not argue that we can image the Trinity only in community. This is my addition.

26. Iozzio, "The Writing on the Wall," 63.

27. Iozzio, "The Writing on the Wall," 60–65.

28. Richard Holton, "Memory, Persons and Dementia," *Studies in Christian Ethics* 29, no. 3 (2016): 256–60, at 260.

29. Mary Jo Iozzio, "Radical Dependence and the *Imago Dei*: Bioethical Implications of Access to Healthcare for People with Disabilities," *Christian Bioethics* 23, no. 3 (2017): 234–60, at 244.

30. Rivera, "Thinking Bodies," 216–17.

31. Cristina L. H. Traina, "Integrity, Vulnerability, and Temporality," *De Ethica* 7, no. 3 (2023):30–46, https://doi.org/10.3384/de-ethica.2001-8819.237330.

32. Powell, *The Disabled God Revisited*, 135–36.

33. Powell, *The Disabled God, Revisited*, 128–36.

34. Hill Fletcher, *Motherhood as Metaphor*, 211.

35. Eiesland, *The Disabled God*, 102.

36. Personal communication from Richard Kieckhefer, 10/27/2022: "There's a long tradition that all are called to sainthood. But the heroic virtue seen in a saint is at least in tension with the recognition of finitude. The saint takes seriously the demand for perfection that seeks to transcend limits."

37. Spyridoula Athanasopoulou-Kypriou, "Icons as Women's Horizon for Their Becoming Divine in the Eastern Orthodox Church: Exploring the Political Dimensions of Iconology and Iconography," *Journal of the European Society of Women in Theological Research* 19 (2011): 67–78, at 73. Thanks to Rachel Contos for this reference.

38. Athanasopoulou-Kypriou "Icons," 76.

39. Gracie Morbitzer, "The Modern Saints," Etsy (August 7, 2023), https://www.etsy.com/shop/GracieMorbitzer?ref=shop-header-name&listing_id=551390955.

40. For a comprehensive view of the series, see Gracie Morbitzer, "Saints," The Modern Saints (August 7, 2023), https://www.themodernsaints.com/all-saints.

41. Elizabeth A. Johnson, CSJ, *Friends of God and Prophets* (New York: Continuum, 1998), 220.

42. Louth, *Introducing Eastern Orthodox Theology*, 113.

43. "St. Teresa of Avila," Carmelite Sisters of Ireland (August 7, 2023), https://www.carmelitesisters.ie/st-teresa-of-avila/.

44. The case for Dorothy Day's official sainthood is in process. But, as this process confirms popular belief in a person's sanctity rather than bestows it, I count her among the saints.

45. Peter Anthony Mena, "Scenting Saintliness: The Ailing Body, Chicana Feminism, and Communal Identity in Ancient Christianity," *Journal of Feminist Studies in Religion* 33, no. 2 (2017): 5–20, at 18.

46. Stamatis Skliris, *In the Mirror: A Collection of Iconographic Essays and Illustrations* (Alhambra, CA: Western American Diocese of the Serbian Orthodox Church, 2007), cited in Athanasopolou-Kypriou, "Icons," 73–74.

III. FINITUDE, GENDER, AND PREGNANCY

1. M. Shawn Copeland, *Knowing Christ Crucified: The Witness of African American Religious Experience* (Maryknoll, NY: Orbis, 2018), 130.

2. Mayra Rivera Rivera, "Thinking Bodies: The Spirit of a Latina Incarnational Imagination," in *Decolonizing Epistemologies: Latina/o Theology and Philosophy*, ed. Ada-María Isasi-Díaz and Eduardo Mendieta (New York: Fordham University Press, 2011), 223.

3. Thanks to Rachel Contos for this reference.

4. Rivera, "Thinking Bodies," 223.

5. Elizabeth Arias, Betzaida Tejada-Vera, Kenneth D. Kochanek, and Farida B. Ahmad, "Provisional Life Expectancy Estimates for 2021," *National Vital Statistics System Vital Statistics Rapid Release* 23 (August 2022), https://www.cdc.gov/nchs/data/vsrr/vsrr023.pdf.

6. See Margaret Farley, "Ethics, Ecclesiology, and the Grace of Self-Doubt," in Farley, *Changing the Questions: Explo-*

rations in Christian Ethics, ed. Jamie L. Manson (Maryknoll, NY: Orbis, 2015), 143–60.

7. See, for instance, Sarah MacDonald and Nicole Symmonds, "Rioting as Flourishing? Reconsidering Virtue Ethics in Times of Civil Unrest," *Journal of the Society of Christian Ethics* 38, no.1 (2018): 25–42.

8. See, for example, Congregation for Catholic Education, "'Male and Female He Created Them': Towards a Path of Dialogue on the Question of Gender Theory in Education" (Vatican City: Vatican Press, 2019), https://www.vatican.va/roman_curia/congregations/ccatheduc/documents/rc_con_ccatheduc_doc_20190202_maschio-e-femmina_en.pdf; United States Conference of Catholic Bishops Committee on Doctrine, "Doctrinal Note on the Moral Limits to Technological Manipulation of the Human Body" (March 20, 2023), https://www.usccb.org/resources/Doctrinal%20Note%202023-03-20.pdf; and Pope John Paul II, *Man and Woman He Created Them: A Theology of the Body*, trans. Michael Waldstein, new trans. based on the John Paul II archives (Boston: Pauline Books & Media, 2006).

9. For instance, see Uri Gneezy, Kenneth L Leonard, and John A. List, "Gender Differences in Competition: Evidence from a Matrilineal and a Patriarchal Society," *Econometrica* 77, no 5. (September 2009): 1637–44, http://gap.hks.harvard.edu/gender-differences-competition-evidence-matrilineal-and-patriarchal-society.

10. Elizabeth A. Johnson, *She Who Is: The Mystery of God in Feminist Theological Discourse* (New York: Crossroad, 1993), 155.

11. This exchange must take different forms with different people. If we know a person well, the answer may be inflected by our experience of the conditions of their

flourishing. For instance, toddlers may signal the need for a nap by asking for a story or a cuddle; dementia patients may respond to a disorienting situation by angrily telling us to leave. Some communications need more translation than others. This is one of the reasons that intimate, respectful care relationships are essential to finite flourishing.

12. Pope Francis, “Risposte del Dicastero a S.E. Mons. Negri” (October 31, 2023), https://www.vatican.va/roman_curia/congregations/cfaith/documents/rc_ddf_20231031-documento-mons-negri.pdf.

13. Sandra Sullivan-Dunbar, *Human Dependency and Christian Ethics* (Cambridge: Cambridge University Press, 2015), 210–18.

14. On decoupling bodily givenness from divine intention, see Madison Chastain, “Fearing Bodies That Change: What Trans Discernment Can Teach Us,” *National Catholic Reporter*, August 4, 2023, https://www.ncronline.org/opinion/guest-voices/fearing-bodies-change-what-trans-discernment-can-teach-us.

15. Rosemary Radford Ruether, *Sexism and God-Talk: Toward a Feminist Theology* (Boston: Beacon Press, 1983), 109–14.

16. Continued listening is essential. For example, medicine has recently become more cautious about hormonal and surgical treatment for children with gender dysphoria, a reminder that questioning and discomfort with one’s apparent gender are not always lasting. But neither is it evidence that everyone with gender dysphoria can overcome it by simply accepting their bodies and their society’s gendered social roles. See, for example, Frieda Klotz, “A Teen Gender-Care Debate Is Spreading across Europe,” *The Atlantic* (April 28, 2023), https://www.theatlantic.com/health/

archive/2023/04/gender-affirming-care-debate-europe -dutch-protocol/673890/.

17. See "2023 Anti-trans Bills Tracker," Trans Legislation Tracker (August 29, 2023), https://translegislation .com/.

18. Brian Fraga, "US Bishops Vote to Revise Health Care Directives on Transgender Patients," *National Catholic Reporter* (June 16, 2023), https://www.ncronline.org/news/ us-bishops-vote-revise-health-care-directives-transgender -patients.

19. See, for instance, Neal McNamara, "Key Schools In Worcester Diocese Decline New Gender, LGBTQ+ Policies," *Patch* (August 16, 2023), https://patch.com/massachusetts/ worcester/key-schools-worcester-diocese-decline-new -gender-lgbtq-policies.

20. Margaret D. Kamitsuka, *Abortion and the Christian Tradition: A Pro-Choice Theological Ethic* (Louisville, KY: Westminster John Knox, 2019).

21. See, for instance, Lisa Tessman, *Moral Failure: On the Impossible Demands of Morality* (New York: Oxford University Press, 2016); Kate Jackson-Meyer, *Tragic Dilemmas in Christian Ethics* (Washington, DC: Georgetown University Press, 2022); and Kate Ward, *Wealth, Virtue and Moral Luck: Christian Ethics in an Age of Inequality* (Washington, DC: Georgetown University Press, 2021).

22. Susan A. Ross, personal communication.

23. As Judith Butler has argued, our precarious residence on the same finite planet means that choosing against an anonymous plea is equally a betrayal because our integral interdependence extends across oceans and not just across the street. See Judith Butler, "Precarious Life, Vulnerabil-

ity, and the Ethics of Cohabitation," *The Journal of Speculative Philosophy* 26, no. 2 (2012):134–51.

24. Rachel Contos, personal communication.

25. Thanks to Rachel Contos for insight into Elizabeth's and Mary's communion of mutual support.

26. Delores S. Williams, *Sisters in the Wilderness: The Challenge of Womanist God-Talk* (Maryknoll, NY: Orbis Books, 1993), 15–31.

27. William Styron, *Sophie's Choice* (New York: Random House, 1979).

28. See M. Antonia Biggs, Heather Gould, and Diana Green Foster, "Understanding Why Women Seek Abortions in the US," *BMC Women's Health* 13, no. 29 (August 29, 2023), https://doi.org/10.1186/1472-6874-13-29.

29. Jackson-Meyer, *Tragic Dilemmas*, 119–23. Jackson-Meyer does not apply this thinking specifically to abortion.

30. See, for instance, Eleanor Klibanoff and Rebecca Schneid, "Tearfully Testifying against Texas' Abortion Ban, Three Women Describe Medical Care Delayed," *The Texas Tribune*, July 19, 2023 (updated July 23, 2023), https://www.texastribune.org/2023/07/19/texas-women-testify-abortion-ban/.

31. See SisterSong Women of Color Reproductive Justice Collective, August 29, 2023, https://www.sistersong.net/; Kimala Price, "It's Not Just about Abortion: Incorporating Intersectionality in Research about Women of Color and Reproduction," *Women's Health Issues* 31, no. 3S (2011): S55–S57; Kimala Price, "What Is Reproductive Justice? How Women of Color Activists Are Redefining the Pro-choice Paradigm," *Meridians: Feminism, Race, Transnationalism* 10, no. 2 (2010): 42–65; Rebecca Todd Peters, *Trust Women: A Progressive Christian Argument for Reproductive Justice* (Boston:

Beacon Press, 2018); and Emily Reimer-Barry, "Another Pro-life Movement Is Possible," *CTSA Proceedings* 74 (2019): 21–41.

32. Bryan Massingale, "The Systemic Erasure of the Black/Dark-Skinned Body in Catholic Ethics," in *Catholic Theological Ethics, Past, Present, and Future: The Trento Conference*, ed. James F. Keenan, SJ (Maryknoll, NY: Orbis, 2011), 92–97, at 95–96; Emilie M. Townes, *Breaking the Fine Rain of Death: African American Health Issues and a Womanist Ethic of Care* (New York: Continuum, 1998), 9–12, 23–25; Jackson-Meyer, *Tragic Dilemmas*, 141–43, 155–57.

33. Massingale, "Systemic Failure," 95.

34. Jackson-Meyer, *Tragic Dilemmas*, 155.

CONCLUSION

1. See Lisa D. Powell, *The Disabled God Revisited: Trinity, Christology, and Liberation* (London: T&T Clark, 2023), 122–24.

2. Robyn Henderson-Espinoza, "Transing Religion: Moving Beyond the Logic of the (Hetero)Norm of Binaries," *Journal of Feminist Studies in Religion* 34, no. 1 (2018): 88–92, at 90–91.

3. Powell, *The Disabled God Revisited*, 137.

4. Elise Ann Allen, "Pope Warns That for Some U.S. Catholics, Ideology Has Replaced Faith," *Crux* (August 29, 2023), https://cruxnow.com/vatican/2023/08/pope-warns-that-for-some-u-s-catholics-ideology-has-replaced-faith.

5. Nancy K. Napier, "The Myth of Multitasking: Think You Can Multitask Well? Think Again," *Psychology Today* (May 12, 2014), https://www.psychologytoday.com/us/blog/creativity-without-borders/201405/the-myth-of-multitasking.

6. William Werpehowski, "In Search of Real Children: Innocence, Absence, and Becoming a Self in Christ," in *The*

Vocation of the Child, ed. Patrick McKinley Brennan (Grand Rapids: Eerdmans, 2008), 53–74 at 55.

7. Daniel P. Horan, *Catholicity and Emerging Personhood: A Contemporary Theological Anthropology* (Maryknoll, NY: Orbis, 2019), 156.

8. Nancy Pineda Madrid, "The Evil of Violence against Women, and the Hope Manifest in Pope Francis' Enduring Legacy," Pope Francis at 10: Enduring Legacy, Future Vision, The Center at Mariandale, Ossining, NY, March 31, 2023.

9. William Walsham How, "For All the Saints Who from Their Labors Rest," 1864.